More Praise for *A Leadership Kick in the Ass*

"Bill Treasurer offers tips from the trenches on how leaders can recover from failure, rejection, and embarrassment—and he manages to make it sound like fun. If you've ever been accused of taking yourself too seriously, this book may be an antidote."
—**Adam Grant, Wharton Professor and** *New York Times* **bestselling author of** *Originals* **and** *Give and Take*

"This book's title may have grabbed your attention, but its core topic—the human ego—is dear to my heart. Using candor and humor in equal measure, Bill Treasurer gets real about the leadership advantages of what I'll just call *effective redirection*. Ha! This book is not just a fun read—it's a wake-up call for leaders at every level."
—**Ken Blanchard, coauthor of** *The New One Minute Manager®* **and** *Collaboration Begins with You*

"Failure may not be fun, but as Treasurer has proven in his rich, in-the-trenches experience in business, you can learn more from one failure than from untold wins. *A Leadership Kick in the Ass* is exactly what you need to pick yourself up, find out what went wrong, and move on, smarter and stronger than ever!"
—**Marshall Goldsmith, Thinkers50 #1 Leadership Thinker in the World**

"*A Leadership Kick in the Ass* is, at its core, about two essential human virtues—courage and humility—and a reminder that these two qualities are inextricably linked. Bill Treasurer shows us that it takes a lot of courage to open yourself up to honest feedback from others and how that openness enables you to become more grounded, more aware, more confident, and more caring. At times Bill is highly irreverent and cheeky, but he's always deeply caring and respectful of the difficult challenges leaders face. And Bill does not simply render critiques; every step of the way he offers insightful and practical advice on how you can lead with your best self. Through stories from his personal and coaching experiences, Bill reveals the transformative power of the courage to be human. This is one of the most unique and valuable books you will read all year, and I highly recommend it."
—**Jim Kouzes, coauthor of the bestselling and award-winning** *The Leadership Challenge* **and Dean's Executive Fellow of Leadership, Leavey School of Business, Santa Clara University**

"Bill artfully describes the harsh, if somewhat humbling, reality that leaders do learn some of the most valuable lessons through mess-ups! The approach Bill uses in taking the reader through poignant examples while offering guidance to seize learning opportunities as they occur is but one of the elements that combine to make this a great read!"
—**Mark Brashear, CEO, John Varvatos**

"Bill Treasurer's over two decades of experience working with leaders comes shining through in this must-read book for all leaders. Bill's no-nonsense approach to calling it as it is, and getting us as leaders to truly look at ourselves with all our 'pimples and warts,' is a refreshing and necessary, albeit sometimes hard, dose of reality we must be willing to face if we truly want to be the best leaders we can. Bill's insights, examples, and action plans throughout the book will help all leaders who have the courage to choose to be better!"
—**Jeff Hayes, President and CEO, CPP, Inc.**

"Bill has taken one heck of a touchy topic and motivates us to read about our foibles and imperfections. Then he has the audacity to challenge us to be better leaders! With just the right amount of advice added to powerful stories, Bill encourages us to be the best leaders we were meant to be."
—**Elaine Biech, author of *Training and Development for Dummies***

"Bill really delivers with this book—a strong message, great storytelling, and lessons that make us take that hard look in the mirror leading to a more authentic self. Finding and leading from this position will undoubtedly bear fruit for readers of this book."
—**Chris Maslin, Director, Biltmore Center for Professional Development**

"Leaders make mistakes. Learning from those mistakes and growing takes courage and humility. For over a decade Bill Treasurer has helped shape our future leaders with his candid, courageous style of training. *A Leadership Kick in the Ass* lights the path to confident, courageous, and inner-centered leadership. I highly recommend this book."
—**Matthew Walsh, Cochairman, The Walsh Group**

"Bill Treasurer reminds us that every leader is flawed. Every leader can improve, learn new lessons, and make different choices. He doesn't let his readers get stale as leaders. His style is warm yet confrontative. A winning combination for real growth."

—**Beverly Kaye, founder and Chair, Career Systems International, and coauthor of** *Love 'Em or Lose 'Em* **and** *Help Them Grow or Watch Them Go*

"Bill Treasurer provides proven tools and processes for managers at every phase of their career to grow and thrive in the midst of their biggest disappointments. A must-read if you're serious about improving your leadership."

—**Karin Hurt, coauthor of** *Winning Well*

"The greatest lessons in life don't come from success. They come from our missteps, setbacks, and screw-ups. This book will help you turn them into invaluable lessons that you'll one day look back on with gratitude for all they taught you. An invaluable resource for any person who wants to be a truly extraordinary leader."

—**Margie Warrell, bestselling author of** *Stop Playing Safe*

"This is a practical book; if you are a leader who hasn't made some big mistakes, you likely aren't leading. This book will help you understand the cause of some mistakes and more importantly help you learn from them. This is a thought-provoking book too; it helps unravel the balance between confidence and humility—an important balance to consider. It's time to start reading."

—**Kevin Eikenberry, bestselling author of** *Remarkable Leadership*

"Bill Treasurer offers a valuable guide to leadership through a series of humorous and honest examples, proving that failures are sometimes the most instrumental lessons on the road to success. Whether you're just getting started in your career or are an established executive, *A Leadership Kick in the Ass* is a pivotal read for anyone who aims to excel as a leader."

—**Pierre Naudé, CEO, nCino**

"Bill's book helps you reframe life's defeats in a way that builds your compassion, your humility, and most importantly, your capacity to get the best out of those that you lead."
—Conor Neill, Professor, IESE Business School, and Past Area Director, Entrepreneurs' Organization

"As in *Courage Goes to Work*, once again Bill Treasurer demystifies a nebulous concept into practical terms. In his newest book, he brings this same level of clarity to 'confidence and humility,' a dynamic tension that effective leaders face. He offers practical insights from real leaders' mistakes, straightforward guidance, and thoughtful reflection. A humorous read on a serious topic that can provide readers with a jolt out of cruise control."
—Julia Urbanchuk, Senior Director, Global Talent & Organization Development, eBay

A Leadership
Kick in the Ass

Other Works by Bill Treasurer

Leaders Open Doors (ATSD, 2014)

Courage Goes to Work

Courageous Leadership:
A Program for Using Courage to Transform the
Workplace (Pfeiffer, 2011)

Positively M.A.D. (Making a Difference)

Right Risk

A Leadership
Kick in the Ass

How to Learn from Rough Landings,
Blunders, and Missteps

Bill Treasurer

BK
Berrett–Koehler Publishers, Inc.
a BK Business book

Berrett-Koehler Publishers, Inc.
1333 Broadway, Suite 1000
Oakland, CA 94612-1921
Tel: (510) 817-2277   Fax: (510) 817-2278   www.bkconnection.com

Ordering Information
Quantity sales. Special discounts are available on quantity purchases by corporations, associations, and others. For details, contact the "Special Sales Department" at the Berrett-Koehler address above.
Individual sales. Berrett-Koehler publications are available through most bookstores. They can also be ordered directly from Berrett-Koehler: Tel: (800) 929-2929; Fax: (802) 864-7626; www.bkconnection.com.
Orders for college textbook/course adoption use. Please contact Berrett-Koehler: Tel: (800) 929-2929; Fax: (802) 864-7626.
Orders by U.S. trade bookstores and wholesalers. Please contact Ingram Publisher Services, Tel: (800) 509-4887; Fax: (800) 838-1149; E-mail: customer.service@ ingrampublisherservices.com; or visit www.ingrampublisherservices.com/Ordering for details about electronic ordering.

Berrett-Koehler and the BK logo are registered trademarks of Berrett-Koehler Publishers, Inc.

Printed in the United States of America

Berrett-Koehler books are printed on long-lasting acid-free paper. When it is available, we choose paper that has been manufactured by environmentally responsible processes. These may include using trees grown in sustainable forests, incorporating recycled paper, minimizing chlorine in bleaching, or recycling the energy produced at the paper mill.

Library of Congress Cataloging-in-Publication Data
Names: Treasurer, Bill, 1962- author.
Title: A leadership kick in the ass : how to learn from rough landings, blunders, and missteps / Bill Treasurer.
Description: First edition. | Oakland, CA : Berrett-Koehler Publishers, Inc., [2017] | Includes index.
Identifiers: LCCN 2016036535 | ISBN 9781626568020 (pbk.)
Subjects: LCSH: Leadership. | Change (Psychology)
Classification: LCC HD57.7 .T735 2017 | DDC 658.4/092—dc23
LC record available at https://lccn.loc.gov/2016036535

First Edition
21 20 19 18 17   10 9 8 7 6 5 4 3 2 1

Book producer: Westchester Publishing Services
Cover designer: Ian Koviak/The Book Designers

To Steve Rivi,
CEO of Aldridge Electric Incorporated,
for leading with integrity, foresight, and courage

Contents

PART IV   Be Humble, Be Good   127

Foreword

Being the manager of a Major League Baseball team has taught me that there are two kinds of leaders: those who have been humbled and those who are about to be. It's not a question of *if* you'll have adversity; it's *when*. Hardship is what makes leadership hard. But facing hardship, and helping others face it too, is pretty much the point of leadership.

Here's what I'd tell a leader who is going through a hard time: welcome to the club! The first time you fail or lose or let people down, it's an initiation, a rite of passage. Now you can stop pretending to be perfect or above the people you're leading. Now you can get out of your own way and start serving others, for real. The humbling of a leader sometimes takes getting the ego kicked out of you.

I'm a little hardheaded, and I held on to my ego too tightly for too long. Life had to clobber me a couple of times before I set aside my pride and paid attention to the lessons hardship was trying to teach me. I've been to the World Series as a player, coach, and manager, and lost each time. I've been called up to the big leagues, and sent back down to the minors. I've been on the cover of *Sports Illustrated*, and to twelve-step recovery meetings (for almost twenty years). Like I tell my players, anything you've done wrong, I've done worse and I've done twice.

The hard knocks I've gone through have been my education. They've taught me that the smallest package in the world is a man wrapped up in himself. As a leader, you've got to tame your ego lest it run roughshod over everyone and everything. I've learned that failure is an event, not a person. As a leader, you can't let failure define you, but you ought to let it shape you and how you lead. Most importantly, I learned that I don't have all the answers. When you're going through hardship, it's silly to try to go it alone. There are people available to us all the time who are eager to help, if we'd just ask. Leaders, like everyone else, need mentors, coaches, and other leaders. Being there for others, especially when they're going through hardship, is a leader's job. It helps if you've been seasoned by some hardships yourself.

As a coach, my job is to help everyone on the team, and the team as a whole, be a little bit better every day. Baseball is a game of wins and losses. All the practice, conditioning, and mental preparation—from preseason through postseason—is focused on one aim: get a lot more Ws than Ls. It's what happens in between games that sets the ledger. If everyone stays focused on doing at least one-tenth of 1 percent better than yesterday, we'll earn more Ws. By striving to be a little better each day, even when things don't go our way, at least we'll have improved.

What I like about *A Leadership Kick in the Ass* is that it is focused on helping you get bigger Ws by learning everything you can from your humbling Ls. The stories have great lessons, and the tips are straightforward and practical. The book's main message is important: good leadership takes confidence and humility. If you're willing to learn, a kick in the backside can bring you both, and you'll be a better leader for it.

The leaders I've gravitated to are strong but not intimidating. They've given me their time, attention, and experience, and helped me want to be better. They've taught me the value of unconditional respect, even when it's hard. I have to respect the umpires, even if I don't agree with the calls. I have to respect the fans, even when they yell at me. I have to respect the media, even when they write bad things about me. I have to respect the great game of baseball, and the greater game of life, even when they're throwing me nasty curveballs. These days, I tell my players, "Respect everything and fear nothing." Everything matters, and everything and everyone deserves respect. The funny thing is, the more respect you give to those around you, the more you'll have for yourself. In good times and in bad, you become a better and more confident leader by respectfully serving others, with humility and gratitude.

Love,
Clint Hurdle
Manager of the Pittsburgh Pirates

Preface

My interest in writing this book began twenty-five years ago, when I learned that I sucked at leading. I was a traveling gypsy, hurling myself off one-hundred-foot towers into small pools at amusement parks throughout North America. I had just become the captain of the U.S. high-diving team and was responsible for leading a troupe of young, high-flying athletes and ensuring that they consistently performed in tip-top shape. It was my first leadership role, and I was a damn good leader, I assumed, because the team was performing decently, and, well, the fact that I had been selected as the team's captain was proof enough.

Each day, my teammates and I would put on a thrilling aerial exhibition for our amusement park patrons. We'd start by performing Olympic-style dives from the three-meter springboard. Next, we performed a comedy routine in which an audience member (another diver, planted in the audience) challenged one of our teammates to a diving competition. After that, we'd entertain the crowd with clown dives—called *dillies*—like the "Baby Catch," when one diver does a front somersault into the arms of another diver, who simultaneously does a back somersault before they crash into the water together. The show culminated with a diver scaling a one-hundred-foot-high diving ladder and hurling himself toward the water, traveling at speeds in excess of fifty miles an hour before hitting a small pool that was ten feet deep.

We were young and cocky, and I was the cockiest among them. I wore my Speedo proudly.

One day, after what I thought was a lousy performance, as the park guests were exiting the aqua theater I lit into the team. "That show was a total disaster," I barked. "Good God, you call that diving? You looked like flying polka dancers. If this is the kind of team I'm saddled with, I have serious concerns about the park extending our contract."

There was something else that had irked me. One of the divers had left his sunglasses on the stage prior to the show. The captains who had taught me would have never stood for that. "One more thing. Who's the idiot who left his stupid shades on the stage for everyone to see?"

Silence.

"Listen up. The next show better be the best one we've ever done, or I'm going to start pruning the team. I'm not going to let you embarrass me like that."

There, I thought, *that'll teach 'em. A swift kick in the ass will do this team some good.*

As the team shuffled away, one of my divers, Steve Willard, stayed behind. Steve was older than me, and had seemed less fazed during my previous outbursts with the team. Once the team was out of earshot, Steve said, "Let me tell you something, Treasurer: if you keep talking down to us, I'll walk. I don't need this job so badly that I'm willing to let you treat me and everyone else like crap."

I became defensive. Who was he to talk to me like that? I thought. If I let him dominate me, people will see me as weak. "Hey, I'm your boss, not the other way around. I'll treat you and the team like you deserve to be treated. If you want me to stop yelling, earn it by performing the way I expect you to."

Steve shook his head like I was missing something. "Listen, dude. You've got bigger problems than the sunglasses I forgot on the stage. If you keep making people afraid of you, nobody is going to want to work for you. You suck at leading."

Gandhi once said, "The truth only hurts if it should." Steve's harsh comments stung because, down deep, I knew they were true. I wasn't being a leader; I was being a jerk. I sucked at leading. The truth was, I didn't know what I was doing. I had no idea who I was as a leader. The best I could do was mimic the leadership style of the captains I had watched, other bosses before them, and ultimately my dad. My own approach to leadership was mostly based on the heavy-handed, high-strung, and disciplinarian style of my father. I wasn't being me. I was me being him. *Respect me, dammit, or else!*

Leadership change often requires a startling blow, and Steve's words were the jolt I needed and deserved. I was utterly humiliated. After licking my wounds of embarrassment, I set out to become a better leader. I started reading books on leadership, observing leaders I admired, trying different leadership approaches, and paying close attention to the needs and reactions of my divers. Respect, I learned, can't be forced or commanded. It has to be earned and re-earned through every encounter with those whom you're leading. The more I explored my interest in leadership, and the more focused I became on earning the team's respect, the better I got at leading. Eventually, I decided to go to graduate school, and I did my thesis on the relationship between leadership style and effectiveness.

Humiliation is powerful, important, and revealing. It strips away the layers of defensiveness that our egos devote so much time to building and fortifying. To be humiliated is to be vulnerable, exposed, and defenseless . . . all things the ego vigilantly guards against. What makes the experience of being humiliated so valuable to a leader's development is that it is through humiliation that one gains humility. And humility is crucial to leadership.

How I Get My Kicks

In the two decades since retiring as a high diver, I've been a practitioner of leadership development. My professional life now consists of working with experienced and emerging leaders, designing and delivering comprehensive leadership development programs (often multiyear in nature), coaching executives one on one, delivering leadership keynotes, and writing leadership-related books. I am privileged to have spent nearly every working day over the last twenty years as a developer of leaders. It's what I do.

I have great respect for leadership authors who study leadership at major universities, and I often apply what I've learned from them in my work. Their research makes an invaluable contribution to the study and practice of leadership. But I am no leadership scholar. I am a leadership plumber. Instead of studying leadership from high on a university hill, I show up to the job site every day, roll up my sleeves, and work directly with leaders to remove whatever hairballs may be mucking up their leadership pipes. The work ain't always pretty.

In the pages that follow, I'll share stories and insights that come directly from my daily work with leaders. There won't be any research statistics or academic theories. Instead, the lessons will draw from the most ancient form of research: personal experience. The lessons in this book come directly from the work I've done with thousands of leaders around the globe. One theme in particular will be reinforced throughout the book: that the greatest leadership lessons—and the development of your unique leadership identity—come from mistakes, embarrassment, and humiliation. The most enduring and transformative leadership lessons result from a good kick in the ass.

Time and time again in my work with leaders, I have heard stories of transformational change that hinged on a jarring event. Consider a few examples:

➤ Over the course of three months, a middle manager has two out of six direct reports quit. HR informs the manager that during exit interviews each person cited being micromanaged by the manager as the reason for his or her departure. Ouch!

➤ A department director becomes deeply frustrated that she hasn't made it into the VP ranks, where she argues she belongs. Finally, the CEO tells her why she's been excluded: the VPs see her as uncooperative and contentious, and they just don't like working with her. Ouch!

➤ A hotshot new leader goes through his first 360-degree feedback survey and is dumbstruck when he reads that he is "arrogant" and "obnoxious." Ouch!

➤ An experienced senior partner who is up for the managing partner role gets passed over for a colleague. After interviewing her prior employees, the selection committee decides against the promotion because she "lacks loyalty" and doesn't "bring people along with her." Ouch!

➤ A project manager has an epiphany that work has become an unhealthy obsession after leading a conference call with her team . . . two hours after delivering a baby. Ouch!

➤ Over the course of a decade, a senior leader champions the career of a trusted direct report whom he views as his most likely successor. The leader, who prides himself on being a good judge of character, is shocked to discover that his direct report has been running a side business with his executive assistant . . . with whom he is having an affair. Ouch!

A Leadership Kick in the Ass explores how startling experiences—often in the form of embarrassing or humiliating events—can have a powerful impact on your development as a leader.

From Bad to Good

The untold truth about leadership is that good leaders nearly always start out as bad leaders. The path for most leaders isn't from *good* to *great*; it's from *decidedly bad* to *pretty good*. Leadership stripes are earned the hard way. You'll make lots of mistakes, render lots of poor decisions, make lots of political blunders, and suffer through many kicks to the backside. You'll learn how to do things right by doing a lot of things wrong. Eventually, if you allow yourself to learn from the hardship, you develop wisdom. That hard-earned wisdom brings value to your leadership . . . and gray hairs to your head. The trick is to do as little damage as possible while your hardships are investing in your wisdom.

Thanks, I Needed That!

I've never lost sight of the fact that I got interested in the topic of leadership because I was such a sucky leader. Today I am grateful for the steel-toed boot that Steve Willard bruised my oversized ego with all those years ago. That psychological spanking gave me my career, and, ultimately, led to the writing of this book. It was the instigation that pushed me to become a better leader. Though I can't claim to be humble (it seems unhumble to make such a claim), I am much less arrogant than I used to be. I am also much more comfortable in my own skin. A leadership kick in the ass, if you let it, can be the pivotal moment when your leadership style becomes more real, grounded, and effective. If you follow the lessons all the way through, you become a stronger and more confident leader. That's right, humiliation can be the gateway for the development of true confidence. Good leadership often starts with a swift kick in the ass.

Kicking Leadership's Gluteus Maximus

Good judgment is the result of experience and
experience is the result of bad judgment.

—Mark Twain

At some point, every leader is confronted with the reality that his or her leadership is seriously and substantially flawed. It is at this precise moment when a leader faces a choice: learn and grow or remain blindly loyal to ignorance. All leaders worth their salt will get a psychological kick in the rear end eventually. It is a critical and inevitable part of the leadership experience. Choosing to learn from the experience requires exploring the leader you've become and clarifying the leader you want to be. It also involves suffering through temporary embarrassment and insecurity. As the renowned psychologist Carl Jung said, "There is no coming into consciousness without pain."

Some leaders refuse to accept any culpability when they get kicked, choosing to double down on their conviction that their way of leading is "right," regardless of how the people they're leading respond to their leadership. They view the kick not as a learning experience to embrace, but

I

as an insult to reject. While this choice skirts the psychological discomfort that growth requires, the end result is often self-righteousness, rigidity, and leadership narcissism. Ultimately, though, failing to accept and learn from a backside jolt is as futile as trying to keep a beach ball under water. No matter how often a leader rejects feedback that runs counter to his self-identity, the beach ball will keep popping back up in the form of negative consequences. The leader who gets fired from a dozen companies rather than capitulate and accept that his approach to leading needs to change will end up having a lot of empty seats at his retirement party.

How leaders deal with, or fail to deal with, butt-kick moments will make all the difference toward their future effectiveness, impact, and well-being as leaders. In fact, a good old-fashioned kick in the tail can be the turning point in one's career—the moment at which a leader stops swimming against the tide of his limitations. After a gigantic and very public psychological ass kicking, involving getting sacked from the company he founded, Steve Jobs said, "Getting fired from Apple was the best thing that could have ever happened to me."

Confidence, Humility, and Balance

The best leaders, those we most admire, are comfortable in their own skin and help us become more comfortable in ours. The best leaders are centered, grounded, and nontoxic. They lead not so their power can grow, but so ours can. Through giving the best of themselves, they draw out the best in us. The best leaders are confident and humble, and in balanced proportions. The goal of this book is to help you grow from whatever kicks you may endure so that you can lead from a place of confidence and humility. More than ever, the world needs more confidently humble leaders.

Much of this book centers on confidence, humility, and the balance between the two. They are like siblings, forever bonded, each existing in relation to the other. Each matters to leading, and the absence of one has a crushing impact on the other two. Too much confidence causes a leader to get too far out over his skis, leading to a wipeout. Too much humility can lead to timidity, weakness, and leadership impotency. We want our leaders to display both confidence and humility, but not too much of either. When the two become wildly out of balance, the needs of those being led get sacrificed at the altar of leadership dysfunction.

Functional and Dysfunctional Leadership

We consider leaders functional when they carry the right blend of confidence and humility. Conversely, we view leaders who are excessively one or the other as dysfunctional. The leaders we most want to follow know who they are and what they stand for, yet are also gracious and not stuck up.

The best leaders are centered, grounded, and nontoxic. They lead not so their power can grow, but so ours can.

When confidence becomes untethered from humility, arrogance follows. Arrogant leadership is selfish leadership, and arrogant leaders fixate on getting *their* way. Without the moderating effect of humility, confidence slips into conceit and self-centeredness. The self-centered leader loses sight of the very purpose of leadership: to improve the conditions of those being led. Unless he gets his way, he will be irritable, combative, and controlling.

If confidence minus humility equals arrogance, then humility minus confidence equals weakness. Whereas arrogant leaders are selfish and insist on getting their way, weak leaders are ineffective, ceding the way to more dominant or persuasive people. Weak leaders lack backbone, influence, and ultimately relevance. In the worst instances, weak leaders are useless. They don't get things done. They don't effect change. They don't wield influence. Few things are as pitiful as an impotent and irrelevant leader. Nobody wants to be led by a wuss.

The Rude Awakening

Eventually, arrogance and weakness lead to the same outcome: a humiliating wake-up call for the leader. Ass kicks are startling and embarrassing experiences, often brought on by the leader's own behavior. They are the natural consequences of overly strong or anemically weak leadership. Leaders mature, progress, and evolve based on how they respond to hurtful moments. This book provides practical guidance to ensure that you benefit whenever you get your butt kicked. By exploring the concepts of confidence and humility—as well as other important leadership concepts like self-respect, selflessness, and resilience—the book aims to help you be a more functional leader. Or, at the very least, the book will help you minimize the impact of your leadership dysfunctions!

Leadership with Pimples and Warts

I need to be clear right up front that I have no intention of dressing up leadership with a rosy veneer. My work with leaders has convinced me how immensely difficult it is to get leadership right. Leading other people, for a host of reasons that we'll explore, is really, really hard. Indeed, the sheer glut of leadership books may be the best evidence of how hard leadership truly is. If it were easy, budding leaders wouldn't be so thirsty for leadership advice. Rather than try to glamorize the topic, I intend to strip it down, so you can have a more grounded, authentic, and reality-based view of what it takes to lead. Unlike other leadership books you may have read, *A Leadership Kick in the Ass* proposes that

➤ leadership is easier to get wrong than to get right,
➤ leaders are often their own worst enemies, and often get in their own ways,
➤ the most enduring and transformative leadership lessons come from humiliating leadership experiences well navigated,
➤ not everyone is cut out to lead (but everyone can grow in their leadership influence),
➤ to be most effective, leaders need both confidence *and* humility; deficiencies in either cause poor or damaging leadership.

This probably isn't the first book about leadership that you've picked up to read. Nor is it the first leadership book

I've written. My hope, though, is that it will be the first leadership book that pushes you forward with a footprint on your bum. If you read this book and nothing about your leadership changes, then I haven't done my job as an author. You won't change if all I give you is leadership platitudes and niceties. Your brain doesn't need any more leadership cotton candy. Rather, the book's aim is to rattle you, provoke you, and challenge you. So along the way, and at the end of each chapter, I'll give you a little kick so that the concepts sting enough to hold you accountable to your leadership potential. To write a book about the importance of butt kicks and then not give you any would be out of step with the book's message, don't you think?

A good ass kick can provoke a great comeback. Sprinkled throughout the book are stories about people who succeeded not in spite of their kicks, but because of them. These stories are under the heading "Kickass Comebacks," and I included them to inspire great comebacks from you, too.

A Word on the Word

It took a while to settle on the title of this book. My publisher and I considered easier, softer words. In the end, though, we settled on a three-letter swear word. Why? Because of the truth of the word. Sometimes situations are just so perplexing, embarrassing, and leveling that they kick your ass. I mean, haven't you ever heard someone describe a situation as being so upsetting that it's "kicking my ass"? Sure you have. Maybe you've even said the words yourself. That said, I promise not to toss the word around like a New York City dockworker. Besides, you're not a *Mayflower* pilgrim, right?

Consider, too, that the phrase has a strong positive connotation. When you talk about wanting to give someone a good kick in the fanny, it's to inspire change, help someone perform to his or her potential, and inspire accountability. It's a way of kick-starting positive action and forward movement.

Finally, it may help to know that my eighty-year-old mother approved of the word, saying, "Let's be honest, Bill, *ass* isn't really much of a swear word."

Nobody wants to be led by a wuss.

This Kick's for You

In particular, you'll get a lot out of *A Leadership Kick in the Ass* if you're still smarting from the last you had. In other words, if you're a leader who has been humiliated by a recent hardship or failure, this book is for you. You'll also benefit from the book if you're

> ➤ someone who is new to the leadership ranks—a rookie or a greenhorn,
> ➤ an experienced leader who is moving into a new or substantially bigger role,
> ➤ a participant in a leadership development program, or a leader going through a 360-degree feedback process,
> ➤ a recently fired executive who is suffering from a crisis of confidence or questioning your ability to lead,

➤ an experienced leader who has become disillu-
sioned with how massively hard and perplexing
leading others has turned out to be.

You know who else can benefit from this book? Know-it-
all leaders who think they've got the topic all figured out,
and that they have nothing left to learn about leadership.
In other words, leaders whose bloated egos could use
some downsizing. These folks might want to put on their
Kevlar underwear!

How the Book Holds Together

Chapter	You'll Learn	Key Takeaways
Preface	How this book was twenty-five years in the making	➡ The greatest leadership lessons come in the form of a startling jolt ➡ Humility is an outcome of humiliation
Introduction: Kicking Leadership's Gluteus Maximus	What this book is about, and why it's time to strip down leadership's veneer and get real about leadership	➡ You'll be deemed a functional or dysfunctional leader by how you handle your startling moments
Part I: Transformative Humiliation Underscores the importance of "transformative humiliation," and explores how butt kicks typically work		
Chapter 1: Ain't That a Kick in the Pants	Why your response to a butt kick will determine whether you benefit from it	➡ Self-discovery takes courage ➡ Kicks shine a light on our shadows . . . and that's a good thing

Chapter	You'll Learn	Key Takeaways
Chapter 2: The Anatomy of a Butt Kick	Why the more oblivious you are before the kick determines how painful the kick will be	➡ There are four stages that butt kicks go through ➡ Accepting or rejecting your kick results in either humility or arrogance
Part II: Career Kicks Describes the kinds of kicks you're likely to experience at different stages in your career		
Chapter 3: Kick Me, I'm New!	How butt kicks help new leaders get experience	➡ New leaders quickly face startling realities ➡ The most important shift leaders make is from self*ish*ness to self*less*ness
Chapter 4: The Cheeky Middle	Why midcareer kicks are so painful, and how they can influence the kind of leader you'll be if you make it to the senior ranks	➡ Midcareer leaders are often frustrated by a specific type of tension ➡ Common midcareer kicks include the Passover, the Smack-down, and Ebbing
Chapter 5: Shrinking Big Shots: Seasoned Leaders Getting Their Kicks	Why leadership season-ing and wisdom are functions of accumulated butt-kick lessons applied	➡ Cresting and the fear of closing doors makes seasoned leaders feel marginalized ➡ The entire workforce can benefit from senior leader "ambassadors"
Part III: Leading, for Worse or for Better Introduces two leadership archetypes that are particularly prone to getting kicked: Pigheads and Weaklings. Also sets *confident humility* as leadership's highest behavioral aspiration.		
Chapter 6: Kick-Worthy Leaders: Pigheads and Weaklings	How arrogance and weakness are signs of poor leadership, and how both lead to an ass kicking	➡ There is a difference between self-respect and self-neglect

(continued)

(continued)

Chapter	You'll Learn	Key Takeaways
Chapter 7: A More Perfect Derrière: Confident Humility	How embarrassing events can ultimately result in confident humility, and why possessing both should be the highest behavioral aspiration of all leaders	➡ Over- and underconfidence is imbalanced leadership ➡ Having a right-sized ego is more important than having a big or small one
Chapter 8: Three Expressions of Confident Humility	How confidence and humility can be used to help you become versed in three leadership roles: Loyal Rebel, Velvet Hammer, and Genuine Faker	➡ Loyalty works best when matched with independence ➡ Assertiveness works best when matched with diplomacy ➡ Sometimes the right approach is to fake it till you make it
Part IV: Be Humble, Be Good Provides strategies and tips for kicking your own duff so that you can keep your ego in check. Culminates with a vision of what leadership can look like after you've applied all of the lessons your humiliating event aims to teach you.		
Chapter 9: How to Kick Your Own Ass	How a consistent regimen of self-inflicted butt kicks will keep you self-aware, and prevent others from having to kick you	➡ Leadership takes self-discovery, and self-discovery takes courage ➡ You grow by purposefully doing uncomfortable things ➡ Every leader should have a chief ego deflator
Chapter 10: Leading at the Point of Goodness	How being a good leader starts with being a good person	➡ Integrity matters most to leadership ➡ Good leaders know and live their values ➡ The people you're leading deserve for you to be good

Startling Change

Heavyweight boxer Mike Tyson famously once said, "Everybody has a plan until they get punched in the mouth." By definition, a swift kick in the ass is painful. Essential as they are to the leadership maturation process, the learning starts after you pick yourself up off the mat. A leadership kick in the tuckus can be the moment where everything changes for you as a leader. These stark and startling moments can rattle your confidence to the core, often provoking serious thoughts of rejoining the nonleader ranks or quitting altogether. But these moments can also be the starting point where you assess your strengths, clarify your values, and develop an authentic and true leadership voice and style. Ass-kick moments are important because they can make you set aside a false leadership identity so that a more genuine and grounded identity can emerge. These events have the potential to inspire what I call *transformative humiliation*, and when that transformation happens, you'll be more respectful of yourself and those around you. Thus, your leadership experiences preceding the kick are just a prelude to the real leadership story that begins afterward.

Transformative humiliation refers to the positive behavioral changes that result from experiences that are embarrassing, leveling, and painful. Properly navigated, such experiences can cause you to become more grounded, real, and humble, resulting in a leadership style and approach that are more uniquely your own. Transformative humiliation is often the entry point for genuine humility and positive leadership change.

Above all, benefiting from *A Leadership Kick in the Ass* requires choosing adaptability over obstinacy. It means assuming responsibility for your own actions and the consequences they bring. It involves having the courage to soberly acknowledge the leader you are today while you diligently work to be a better leader tomorrow. It means heeding the pure voice of your conscience. It means accepting the challenge of personal change and letting go of outdated preconceptions. As Viktor Frankl once said, "When we can no longer change a situation, we are challenged to change ourselves."

The core of this book is really about *independence*. Once you've juiced out all the lessons that your kick hits you with, you'll be unencumbered by doubt and self-consciousness. You won't be dependent on the validation of others to judge your worth as a leader. You'll stop overcompensating for your weaknesses by being falsely confident and overdominant, and, instead, will gain strength in the humble recognition that leading and influencing others is a privilege to be honored and treasured. Your kick will ultimately teach you that the only way to bring out the best in those you're leading is to lead with the best of yourself.

Gaining leadership independence hinges on understanding, anticipating, and contending with the harsh experiences that bruise your ego. That's what this book will help you do. As you'll come to learn, butt kicks are really gifts that can make your leadership more authentic, effective, enjoyable, and wonderfully liberated.

The only way to bring out the best in those you're leading is to lead with the best of yourself.

PART I

Transformative Humiliation

It takes a lot to provoke personal change. Willpower alone hardly ever works. Broken diets, resolutions, and promises bear witness to that. Something more powerful and disruptive is needed to make change take hold: a psychological butt whopping. Sometimes it takes a startling and rude awakening, often accompanied by strong feelings of embarrassment, to bring about enduring change. Pain is often a better teacher than comfort. Why? Because once you've experienced it, you work harder not to experience it again. It's after you fall off a bike and scrape your knees that you pedal harder and faster. Pain commits you to making changes to avoid more pain.

In this section, you'll learn

➤ why embarrassing moments are so important to the growth, development, and seasoning of leaders,

➤ how leaders, through their behaviors and actions, often cause their own butt kicks,

➤ how your reaction to your swift kick will determine whether or not you'll ultimately draw value from it,

➤ how butt kicks work, and why the intensity of the sting is related to how oblivious you are before the kick happens,

➤ what to do the next time you get kicked in the keister!

The primary takeaway from this section is that, when you're a leader, suffering through an embarrassing experience can inspire positive and lasting leadership change.

CHAPTER 1

Ain't That a Kick
in the Pants

Isn't it funny how obvious and oblivious are so close?
—Author unknown

M y work with leaders sometimes involves inviting the leader's direct reports to purposely kick him or her in the keister. One of the most effective ways of doing this is having the leader go through a 360-degree feedback process, where the people they are leading rate the leader's style and performance. The raters often include the leader him- or herself and the leader's boss(es), peers, and direct reports—hence a "360-degree" view. The feedback uses an anonymous survey consisting of quantitative data and qualitative (open-ended) questions. The idea is that people are likely to give more honest answers if they don't feel threatened that the leader will retaliate against them for their honesty. A leader's self-perception can be quite biased, so involving the broader perspective of others can be a useful development tool. While 360-degree surveys aren't perfect, having administered hundreds of them over the years, I've seen them result in positive leadership change. Sometimes dramatically so.

To be sure, it takes courage to subject oneself to a leadership 360. The feedback can be raw and hurtful. In rare instances raters will use the process as a way to get back at a leader they don't like. But mostly the feedback is helpful because it allows the leader to illuminate blind spots that may be blocking his or her effectiveness.

Sometimes Even a Butt Kick Won't Work

Meet Bruce. Bruce is a headstrong senior executive in the construction industry. He is physically imposing (six foot four) and socially dominant. He is the proverbial bull in the china shop, viewing nearly every interaction with clients, subcontractors, and direct reports ("subordinates") as a competition to be won. While Bruce has developed a strong track record of taking on the toughest and most complex projects, he also has a well-earned reputation as a controlling hard-ass who has left a trail of human wreckage in his wake.

As is often the case with leaders like Bruce, a lot of pent-up frustration spewed forth in his 360. Though he rated himself nearly perfect on every leadership question (giving himself nines and tens on a ten-point scale), the people rating him gave him ones and twos. The qualitative comments were just as bad, including one from his boss, who called him "petulant" and "irrational." One direct report called him a "blockhead," and another said he was a "brute."

Less surprising than the stark feedback was Bruce's reaction to it. He basically blew it off. He dismissed it as sour grapes from mediocre performers. It wasn't him, it was *them*! They were just slackers and complainers who couldn't keep up. And if it weren't for *him*, nothing would get done. Even when slapped with overwhelming and illuminating evidence of the need for Bruce to change, he chose to stay obnoxiously loyal to his ignorance. *Blockhead* was an apt description!

Thank You, Sir! May I Have Another?

Now meet Derek. Like Bruce, Derek works in the construction industry but for a larger company. He is a senior project manager who typically leads large civil engineering projects such as water treatment plants and hydroelectric dams. Derek's 360 was even more scathing than Bruce's. Words that popped out of his report included *hot-tempered*, *explosive*, *unapproachable*, *aggressive*, *edgy*, *harsh*, and *impersonal*. Rater comments included the following:

> ➤ *Derek's a good talker and not a good listener. He will cut you off before you can finish making a point.*
> ➤ *He has a habit of self-promoting and blowing his own horn.*
> ➤ *He cuts people down in a derogatory way . . . often in front of other people.*

To be sure, the feedback stung Derek. At first he got a little defensive. Then he got quiet. Then he got inquisitive, asking, "How do these results compare to my peers?"

"Not too well," I confessed.

After more silence, he said, "Okay. What do I need to do?"

"Get to work," I replied.

For the next six months Derek and I spent ninety minutes every other Tuesday focused on improving his leadership. He'd use his own work situations as a petri dish to experiment with different approaches. He'd have small homework assignments, such as thinking about leaders who had left a positive and/or negative impression on him, reading leadership articles, and clarifying the kind of leader he would be proud to be. He also kept a leadership journal, reflecting on such questions as, "Why, exactly, do you want to lead others?" "What, exactly, qualifies you to lead others?" and "In what ways, exactly, would you like to make a positive difference in the lives of those whom you lead?" The key was for Derek to get as specific as possible. Hence the heavy emphasis on the word "exactly."

During our coaching sessions it also became clear that lack of self-care was an issue. Beyond work, he didn't have a life. All he did was work. He didn't make time to work out, he had no social life, and he was full of anxiety. It was easy to see why people didn't like working for him—he was a tightly coiled ball of stress, on the verge of springing loose at any moment. So we made caring for himself (*self-leadership*) a top priority, including joining a gym and setting aside an hour of uninterrupted "me time" at least twice a week.

Becoming a healthier, stronger, and more effective leader takes a genuine investment in yourself. Even still, the payoffs aren't instantaneous. While Derek made real improvements during our coaching time, I didn't learn how fully he had grown until some five years later. One of the advantages of having long-term consulting relationships with my leadership development clients is that I get to work with successive generations of leaders. Often the new leaders who are participating in a leadership program today were led by leaders who went through the program years before. I had originally met Derek when he was a participant in a two-year leadership program I had developed for his company. Five years after completing the program, two of Derek's direct reports got accepted to the same program. Both of them talked about what a great mentor he had become for them, how he was a positive influence on their careers, and how they hoped to lead like him someday. In my work with leaders, few things are as gratifying to hear as how a leader with whom you've worked has now become a positive influence on a new generation of leaders. Leadership is really working when leaders create new leaders.

Becoming a healthier, stronger, and more effective leader takes a genuine investment in yourself.

Slapping Cheeks

The difference between the reactions of Bruce and Derek to tough feedback comes down to courage. Not the kind of courage that it takes to fight, compete, or charge a hill, but the kind of courage that it takes to soberly see yourself as you really are. It's courage of a more vulnerable kind. It's the courage it takes to loosen the grip on your need to be right or perfect and admit that you are the main source of your problems and ineffectiveness. This is the courage of capitulation, disarmament, and surrender. Your old ways have lost, and unless you adopt new ways of leading, you will continue to lose over and over again.

This is the courage it takes to own your leadership life. We'll explore this idea further in chapter 9.

Bruce is a grizzled fighter. Throughout his career he succeeded by outdominating and controlling others. He *willed* his way into building hard and complex jobs. Building the job always came first. It's where the money was made. Why should he care what people thought of him? He built the biggest and most profitable projects in the company. His exceptional results *proved* that he was a good leader. Based on Bruce's perspective, it's understandable that he would choose to reject his 360 feedback rather than to accept responsibility for changing.

But in rejecting the feedback of the people who had directly experienced his leadership, Bruce made the deliberate choice not to grow. Choosing otherwise would mean chipping away at his blockhead and cracking open a deeper truth about his successes; the money he made for the company had come at a great cost in human suffering. Yes, Bruce had made a lot of money for the company. But he had also cost the company a lot of money in the form of low morale, high turnover, and lost leadership potential. Not admitting that hard truth was easier than changing. Ultimately, Bruce was a coward. By failing to take responsibility for his leadership failings, he spared himself the discomfort that change causes. By not changing, Bruce was free to do more damage to the people he was charged with leading. Leadership arrogance always exacts a price.

Derek, conversely, took the more courageous path of self-discovery. He soberly looked at the leader he had become and didn't like what he (and others) had seen. He wanted to be a better leader, and that would require adopting a new leadership mind-set and awkwardly trying new leader behaviors. Rather than entrench himself against the marauding feedback invaders like Bruce did, he decided to do the legwork of improving himself. He used the feedback as a baseline against which he could gauge future progress. By using the feedback that way, he evolved from a bad leader to a good one. The difference between Bruce and Derek is that Derek used the lessons drawn from his humiliating 360 feedback to bring about positive leadership changes in himself. In his case, humiliation brought about personal transformation.

Now Discover Your Butt

There's been a lot written about "strength-based" development approaches in recent years. You're better off building on your natural strengths and talents, research suggests, than trying to improve your weaknesses. The usefulness of the strength-based approach explains its popularity. It makes good sense: put yourself in situations where your gifts and talents can be put to good use, and you'll increase the likelihood of being successful. As the great motivational theorist Abraham Maslow said, "A musician must make music, an artist must paint, a poet must write, if he is to be ultimately at peace with himself."

What makes an ass kicking so painful (and useful) is that it shines a red-hot light on the parts of yourself that are holding you back and legitimately need development, often the aspects of yourself that you'd rather avoid or didn't even know existed.

Building on your strengths works best if you have a re-
alistic hold on what your strengths actually are. Pinpointing your strengths takes a careful assessment of the totality
of your makeup, and that includes acknowledging what
you're *not* actually good at. The challenge is that our self-
perception is often rosy or cloudy, causing some people to
highlight the brighter aspects (while minimizing the darker
elements), and others to do the opposite. What makes an
ass kicking so painful (and useful) is that it shines a red-
hot light on the parts of yourself that are holding you
back and legitimately need development, often the aspects
of yourself that you'd rather avoid or didn't even know
existed. Sometimes the kick illuminates the parts of yourself that need pruning or uprooting altogether. Absent the
illumination that the kick provokes, your view of your
strengths is, at best, inaccurate or incomplete.

Sunshine and Shadows

Strengths are good things. Until they aren't. Past a certain
point, our strengths start to cast a shadow. The leader who
is comfortable speaking in public may come to hog attention. The leader who is a gifted critical thinker may become
overly critical of others. The leader who is great interper-
sonally may place too much emphasis on subjective crite-
ria when making decisions.

Every leader should develop and nurture his or her
unique gifts and talents. To be fully developed as a leader,
though, you need to go further. Every leader needs to be
keenly aware that strengths can become overly potent,
sometimes toxically so. The strength of *drive* can give way
to *dominance*, which can become the weakness of *intimi-*

dation. Likewise, the strength of *confidence* can slip over into the weakness of *arrogance.* Every leader is made up of sunshine and shadows. Paying attention only to the shiny parts of your leadership causes your shadow to grow, practically ensuring a kick in the saltshaker.

The ego's first job is self-preservation. In Bruce's case, his ego contributed to his not even being able to look at how his strengths had in fact become weaknesses. Bruce's strength at controlling and dominating the job had spilled over to his controlling and dominating people. While his win-at-all-costs drive contributed to his building big jobs, it also contributed to his losing great people. His competitive zeal resulted in his winning a lot. But it also came at the expense of everyone else around him having to lose. Admitting all that would mean deconstructing everything that, at least in his mind, had made Bruce successful. His ego simply couldn't allow for that. Changing would have required skills that he just didn't have and wasn't ready to learn. It would have meant learning how to be vulnerable, cooperative, and not in control. It would have taken a much harder ass kicking to make Bruce want to change.

And that's exactly what happened. Within two years of going through the 360 process, Bruce got sacked. The people he had led had gotten wiser, older, and less willing to take it. A few of them had themselves moved into leadership positions, and no longer felt the need to subjugate themselves to Bruce's heavy-handedness. People started complaining about Bruce more vocally to the senior executives above him. The din of the mutiny was too loud for his bosses to ignore, so out the door Bruce went. (Of course, in his eyes, it was *their* fault.)

THE SUNSHINE AND SHADOW REVIEW:
A Leadership Team Activity

I t's interesting that the leaders who are charged with bringing out the best in the workforce often struggle with bringing out the best in each other. There is often a surprising amount of game playing at the top of the organization, and in the game of social dominance, leaders often try to outdominate each other. Showing the kind of vulnerability that healthy relationships require can be a challenge for senior leadership teams. One activity that can promote safe vulnerability among the members of leadership teams is "Sunshine and Shadows." Here's how it works:

■ Tell the group that often what we call "weakness" is really just an overgrowth of our "strengths."

■ Have one of the leaders sit in the seat at the head of the table—the "hot seat." In round-robin fashion, have each of the other leaders comment on the strength that the hot-seat leader contributes to the team—his or her "sunshine."

■ After each leader has commented, the hot-seat leader must say, "Thank you." After thanking the group, the leader can ask questions for clarity if he or she wishes.

■ Next, have each leader comment on the "shadow" that is sometimes cast when the hot-seat leader's strength becomes too potent.

■ Again, after each leader has commented, the hot-seat leader must say "Thank you" before asking questions for clarity. He or she may NOT, under any circumstances, offer excuses for, or defenses of, his or her shadow.

■ Once the leader has had his or her sunshine and shadows reviewed, move on to the next leader on the team.

■ After all leaders have gone through the process, have the group discuss the value of understanding each team member's sunshine and shadows.

Here is one fundamental truth about a butt kick: if you refuse to learn the lessons it can provide, a harder and more painful kick is sure to follow. As the saying goes, "If you don't learn the lesson, you have to repeat the class."

How to Handle a Kick in the Butt

How does what you read about Bruce and Derek relate to you? Think back to the last time you learned a lesson the hard way. How did you react? Did you make changes to become better and stronger? Or did you entrench yourself in the conviction of your rightness? Here are some quick tips for ensuring that you're ready to benefit from whatever kicks you may next endure:

> ➤ **Focus on the long game.** A kick is just a momentary speed bump on your longer leadership career. The spike in pain will eventually yield to worthwhile lessons and changes. Focus on where you ultimately want your career to end up, not the detour it may have taken.
> ➤ **Learn from your feelings.** Pay close attention to the feelings that come up for you after you get kicked. Identify what you're feeling, precisely. Do you feel embarrassed, fearful, resentful, or something else? Then ask yourself, "What information is this feeling trying to give me?" and "What is the lesson this feeling is trying to teach me?"
> ➤ **Remember, discomfort = growth.** Comfort may be comfortable, but it's also stagnant. You don't grow in a zone of comfort. You grow, progress, and evolve in a zone of *dis*comfort. The more

uncomfortable the kick feels, the more growth
can result.

➤ **Broaden your view of courage.** Being vulnerable,
open, and receptive to change is a form of courage.
Hard-charging types wrongly see courage as being
fearless. Nothing could be further from the truth.
Courage is fear*ful*. The simplest definition of *courage* is "acting despite being afraid." Courage requires fear. As long as you keep moving forward,
it's when there's a knot in your stomach, a lump in
your throat, and sweat on your palms that your
courage is doing its job.

➤ **Don't be oblivious to yourself.** How much might it
be costing you to remain loyal to your ignorance?
Self-exploration and discovery can be painful, but
what is more painful in the long run is being a
stunted human being, incapable of acknowledging,
assimilating, or shoring up your shortcomings.

➤ **Be your own project.** Lots of people lead projects
better than they lead themselves. Think about what
it takes to lead a great project. You start by identifying your desired outcomes, you put together a
timeline and pinpoint critical milestones, you marshal the resources the project will need to be
successful, and you identify metrics to track progress. Guess what? You can manage your kick
recovery the exact same way.

➤ **Stay present.** Rather than try to avoid all that
surfaces for you during and immediately after the
humiliating event, fully immerse yourself in the
experience. What feelings come up for you? What

fears are at work? How might your feelings and fears serve you once the entire experience plays out? What are you learning and how can you put those lessons to good use?

As much as the self-discovery can be painful, it is also fantastically rewarding. The journey to the center of one's self is the most important voyage you'll ever take. It's how you become a whole person, truly knowing the full dimensions of your talents, idiosyncrasies, and deepest desires.

Ultimately, if you let it, a humiliating kick can be the entry point for a richer, fuller, and more complete understanding of yourself, as a leader and as a human being. Armed with that knowledge, you'll be better able to use your strengths—and actively mitigate the shadows your strengths sometimes cause—so they better serve you and others. Abraham Maslow sums it well: "What is necessary to change a person is to change his awareness of himself."

CHAPTER 2

The Anatomy of a Butt Kick

You may not realize it when it happens, but a kick in the pants may be the best thing in the world for you.
—Walt Disney

M eet Pete. Pete is the director of the IT department of a large suburban hospital. His team is responsible for managing over 150 software applications, providing computer hardware to hospital staff, and ensuring that the hospital complies with state and government security standards. IT failures could be catastrophic to the hospital and the patients it serves. Pete and his team are perpetually under siege with IT demands from nurses, doctors, and administrators. The job is beyond stressful, but he's been at it for over a decade. Being in firefighter mode is nothing new to him. In fact, he seems to do a better job when there are fires to put out.

Pete's team is another story. In the last year, three people have quit, most recently last week. The coder was in the middle of a death-march project that was requiring him to work a lot of weekends and overtime. During his exit interview, he said his wife had given him an ultimatum: either get a new job that allows him to be more present with their three-month-old baby, or get a new wife.

Late on Friday afternoon, Pete's boss, the hospital's CFO, called him into her office. Pete wondered if maybe he was going to get a raise. After all, she had told him numerous times that she appreciates how hard his team works to keep up with the incessant IT demands. On top of that, last year Pete received an "above-and-beyond" award for his leadership on a complicated systems integration program. *I knew my hard work would pay off!* he thinks.

"Let me get right to the point," she said. "Effective today, your services will no longer be needed by the hospital." Her words settled in the air like gunpowder after a fireworks finale. "The hospital appreciates your contributions over the last ten years," she said impersonally.

"Whoa! What?! You've got to be kidding me. Is this a joke?" Pete said, dumbfounded. "What about the above-and-beyond award? What about the ongoing projects I'm leading?"

"I'm sure it's difficult for you. It may be helpful if you reread your last two performance reviews. In particular, the developmental improvement recommendations will be helpful to go over. Now, if you'll excuse me, I have to attend an important meeting of the executive team."

The Four Stages of a Kick

All butt kicks, butt kickers, and butt-kick recipients are unique. That said, hiney-smacking events also share a few common elements. Let's use the example above to deconstruct how a leadership kick in the ass typically works. Each kick has four stages:

1. **Comfortable oblivion:** Prior to getting kicked, you are blind to your own behavior. Life is going swimmingly and you are blithely unaware of the impending insult. Oftentimes you are full of confidence. You can quickly marshal the facts that support the value you're adding to the organization you serve. You view yourself as competent, aware, and deserving. In the case above, Pete walked into the CFO's office oblivious to the kick he was set to receive.

2. **Startling sting:** *Ouch, that hurts!* Butt kicks assault our comfort and, thus, are painful events. As a rule, the more oblivious you are prior to the kick, the more painful the kick will feel. Pete's kick was painful, partly because of his degree of prekick obliviousness, and partly because getting fired is a kick with a serious windup. Most commonly, kicks provoke emotions of fear, anger, rejection, or depression. These emotions often result in defensiveness and self-righteousness—*How dare they kick my ass this way!*

3. **Change choice:** After the sting starts to subside, you are left with a choice. Broadly defined, your choice comes down to *accept* or *reject*. We'll explore this stage in more depth in a moment, because it's the most critical stage in the butt-kick process.

4. **Humility or arrogance:** Depending on the decision you make in stage three, stage four will result in either deeper arrogance or genuine humility. If you double down on your conviction that your kick was an undeserved injustice, you'll fortify your

sense of righteousness. If you take the lumps the kick brings and make changes based on the information that it provides you, you'll exit the butt-kick event with a view of yourself that is more grounded, sober, and humble.

Let's use Pete's example to illustrate how the stages play out. During the first stage, it's easy to see how Pete would start by getting defensive. After all, he had won the above-and-beyond award, validating his worth to the organization. His boss had expressed her appreciation for how hard his team was working. *Damn right they're working hard*, Pete might think, *because I* make *them work hard!*

As mentioned, the more oblivious you are before the butt kick, the harder it hits. Stage one determines the intensity of stage two. In Pete's example, the sting of stage two is made more painful because he didn't see it coming (stage one). He had a vague awareness that there might be issues with his team, but he downplayed their significance. So when he got fired, it hit hard.

Defensiveness is a lagging emotion. It is a *reaction* that is provoked when people feel threatened and afraid. Abrupt kicks jeopardize your sense of identity, your feelings of contentment, and your financial and psychological security. So your ego does what it's supposed to do—it defends you. It's easier, at first, for your ego to come to your defense than for you to accept that something about you needs to change. So the self-preservation part of your brain kicks in and starts to scan your memory catalog to find evidence that invalidates the hard-hitting feedback. *How could this happen to* me! *I'll show them how wrong they are!* is a common refrain. Other postkick refrains include the following:

> ➤ *That's just not true, because . . .*
> ➤ *Well I only did that because . . .*
> ➤ *No, you! You're the one!*
> ➤ *But I'm not the only one to do it—so-and-so does it all the time!*

Given the dramatic and rare nature of Pete's butt kick, it's understandable that he would get defensive. Let's face it: getting fired is a pretty nasty kick in the ass. Unless you're a complete nincompoop, you aren't likely to get fired more than one or two times in the course of your entire career. It's easy to imagine him being steaming mad, calling his friends to vent his anger, and, maybe, contemplating a lawsuit. Pete's ego is in full protection mode. He has been wronged, *dammit*, and his ego will keep reminding him of this over and over. At least initially.

So what should Pete do? At stage three, Pete is left with a critical choice: accept or reject. How he responds during this stage will determine whether the event works for him or against him. Let's review the two change choice options of stage three:

A. Entrench and Defend: If Pete sticks with the view that he is the victim of a wild injustice, he will become the commander in a battle campaign against those whose footprints are on his rear end. He is operating out of a bruised ego. Hence, the more blame he assigns his assaulters, the more his sore ego is assuaged. Making them look bad, his ego believes, will make him look less so. It's a common tactic when adopting an Entrench and Defend approach: shift the focus away from yourself to those who kicked you. The more Pete can make the insult their fault, the less accountability he has to assume. Entrench and Defend is a classic ego-deflection strategy; you protect yourself from the hard work and pain associated with self-discovery by deflecting the fault to others. In a sense, what you're entrenching and defending is your comfortable oblivion—you're trying to get back to the emotional comfort you had before you got your butt kicked. Entrench and Defend is a strategy for reclaiming ignorance by feigning innocence.

B. **Accept, Learn, and Act:** The other option during stage three takes more time and effort. Let's suppose, for example, that after a few days of licking his wounds, Pete follows the CFO's advice and rereads his last two performance reviews. Comments that seemed insignificant when he first got the reviews now have more sting. One paragraph is particularly embarrassing to read: "While your work ethic is commendable, there have been complaints that members of your team are overworked and feel underappreciated. As the team's leader, please pay attention to resource planning so you can manage each team member's workload more thoughtfully. This includes informing me if you need additional resources to meet the team's demand. Finally, a little gratitude will go a long way toward boosting morale during spikes in the team's workload. Learn to say 'Thank you' more generously."

Acceptance takes time to settle in because what you're accepting is fault. It takes a certain capitulation—you have to admit, to yourself at least, your own contribution to the blow. Your mentality shifts from "I was wronged" to "I was wrong." In short, you are giving up your claims of innocence; you are guilty. Acceptance starts with rigorous honesty and ends with sober accountability. It takes *owning it*, in terms of assuming personal accountability for your butt kick, before deep and enduring learning can take place. In Pete's case, he might come to see that his incessant drive for results is connected to strong feelings of inadequacy. While outwardly he portrays confidence, on the inside he has a gnawing sense that he is not quite good enough. Thus, he constantly tries to prove his worth through his output. The more he produces, the less unworthy he feels. Like a man desperately trying to escape emotional quicksand, in order to feel adequately "good enough" he must always be producing *more*. By extension, so must the people who work for him.

Psychologically disruptive experiences like Pete's sometimes require outside perspective from a mentor, coach, or therapist to traverse. It's common to feel ashamed once you realize you actually deserved the ass kicking you got. A neutral third party can help ensure that you don't get subsumed by the heaviness that often accompanies self-examination. A trusted adviser can be a source of encouragement, objectivity, and wisdom. More importantly, a trusted adviser can keep you from beating yourself up.

Aided by a seasoned mentor, Pete can now take action. The options are endless. He might go on a retreat and spend some quality unproductive time just "being."

He might read books on leadership to identify the leader he'd like to be. He might work with a therapist to identify the sources of his feelings of inadequacy so he can move beyond them. He might take up a hobby so that he has a richer outside-of-work identity. One thing he shouldn't do, though, is jump immediately back into a leadership job without fully processing his butt-kick experience.

The Long Arc of the Kick

The choices you make in stage three become the results you get in stage four. Stage four, humility or arrogance, is an outcome. In Pete's case, if he chooses to reject the lessons brought on by his butt kick, say by adopting an Entrench and Defend strategy, he will deepen his sense of righteousness. By doubling down on his ignorance, and by rejecting all accountability for the slap he received, Pete will remain saddled with his feelings of inadequacy. So the behaviors that caused him to get fired in the first place (for example, overworking, being oblivious to the needs of others, ingratitude) will continue to inhibit his effectiveness as a leader in his next leadership role. In fact, they are likely to get worse. Pete's leadership behavior could become more insensitive, obsessive, and eventually ruthless. By refusing to shine the light on his own culpability, the woe-is-me victim who lives inside Pete's soul may grow more self-absorbed and arrogant. *How much longer must I endure all these idiots?!*

If, however, Pete chooses to accept and learn from the lessons his butt kick has to offer, he will see the negative impact that his unreconciled ego issues had on his team.

BEING OBLIVIOUS ABOUT BEING OBLIVIOUS: The Dunning-Kruger Effect

In 1995 McArthur Wheeler rubbed lemon juice all over his face and robbed a bank. Later that same day, after applying more lemon juice, he robbed a second bank.

It turns out that lemon juice has an interesting property. It can be used as invisible ink. If you use lemon juice to write a secret message, the letters only become revealed when exposed to heat. Mr. Wheeler assumed that if he rubbed lemon juice all over his face, his face would become invisible to the banks' security cameras. He had even tested it by taking a selfie with a Polaroid camera (which, evidently, he used incorrectly).

A few hours after the heists, the police got the surveillance tapes and had the local television stations play them on the eleven o'clock news. Within an hour, Mr. Wheeler was identified as the bank robber. Though Wheeler hadn't become invisible, at least he smelled citrusy!

Drawing on Mr. Wheeler's story for inspiration, two psychologists from Cornell University, David Dunning and Justin Kruger, decided to conduct a series of experiments to test how ignorance impacts decision making. After being shown their test scores on assessments of logical reasoning, grammar skills, and humor, students were asked to estimate their own rank in the class. It turned out, the more incompetent a student was, the higher he assumed his rank would be. The converse was also true: the more ability a student had, the more she underestimated her competence. They would also assume that others were as competent as themselves, if not more so.

The Dunning-Kruger effect suggests that the greater your ignorance, the less likely you are to

■ recognize and acknowledge your lack of skill,
■ be aware of the extent of your limitations, and
■ accurately assess the skills of others.

The moral of the story is that the more ignorant you are, the more oblivious you'll be. But there is hope. After receiving training, students were able to assess themselves more realistically. If that doesn't work, may I interest you in a lemon?

Sources: Anupum Pant, "The Astonishingly Funny Story of Mr. McArthur Wheeler," *Awesci*, March 28, 2014, http://awesci.com/the-astonishingly-funny-story-of-mr-mcarthur-wheeler/; and Robert Fisher, "Stupidity for Dummies: The Study of Ignorance Is Helping Us Understand How Intelligence Works," GQ.com, February 14, 2014, http://www.gq-magazine.co.uk/article/stupidity-for-dummies.

He'll realize that it was his own unthoughtful behavior that led directly to his team's unhappiness and disloyalty, which, in turn, led to his getting fired. *Be more thoughtful about others* is a transformational lesson that could change the trajectory of Pete's career (and life) for the better, causing him to be less self-absorbed and more attuned to the needs of the team. He might have and express more gratitude for the sacrifices the team makes. He might become more intentional about balancing their workloads. He likely would be, in short, a better leader. Much more importantly, he would carry the lifelong knowledge that his worth as a human being has very little to do with how productive he is. Worthiness is a function of richness of character, generosity, selflessness, goodness, and leadership.

Either Pete will exit the butt-kicking experience as a more genuinely confident and humble human being, or he will exit as a dominating, self-righteous, overconfident, arrogant jerk. It all comes down to whether Pete accepts or rejects the lessons his butt kick can teach him.

When the Butt Kicking Is Not Your Fault

Not all butt kicks are the result of something you did. But all kicks still follow the four-stage process, and all come with the choice of whether to *accept* or *reject* them. For example, Ken Aldridge is the ex-CEO and current chairman of Aldridge Electric Incorporated, one of the nation's leading civil and electrical contractors. During his tenure as CEO, Ken's impact on the business has been stellar. He has led the company as it has taken on more complex and demanding projects. He has instituted management processes and formalized management roles. He has made smart investments, including acquiring and growing businesses that expanded Aldridge's services, territories, and market reach. And he has launched the company's training and leadership development efforts. He is widely admired inside and outside Aldridge. What makes his story and successes so compelling is that his career as a leader started with a startling wake-up call: his father's fatal heart attack.

Suddenly, Ken was thrust into the CEO role . . . at twenty-seven years old. His father's death was something that he couldn't have predicted, so his stage-one comfort and oblivion prior to the kick were substantial. The pain of the kick (stage two) was almost unbearable. Adding to the personal heartache was the intense pressure of not wanting to let Aldridge's employees down, but feeling ill equipped for the CEO role. His father had been a larger-than-life figure, and Ken, at twenty-seven, had nowhere near the experience his father did.

What choice did Ken really have in stage three but to accept his fate? If he were to reject it, the company would be at serious risk of going under. There was too much at stake and too many people were counting on him for their livelihood. So Ken buckled down and set out to steward the company into the future. He relied heavily on his senior executive team, nearly all of whom were older and more experienced than Ken. He lined up one-on-one visits with customers so he could gain firsthand knowledge of their needs and challenges. He walked the halls and went out to the job sites so he could connect with the employees and field personnel. He invested in his own training and leadership development. Before long, he was establishing his own footprint as CEO.

One of the most significant and long-term results of Ken's butt kick became how he handled his own succession out of the CEO role, years later. Having inherited the business in such a startling way, Ken was much more deliberate than his father had been. Part of Ken's succession strategy was investing heavily in leadership development for all executives and managers so that the company's bench strength is deep. The other part was making sure that his sons inherit the company in a much smoother way than he did. The CEO succession began seven years before Ken moved out of the CEO role, and involves a transitional CEO, Steve Rivi, the company's prior COO. One of Steve's main responsibilities is to prepare Ken's sons, who are now co-COOs, for the eventual transition to the CEO role. Other senior executives, and outside coaches, are also actively involved in the sons' development and preparation.

Of all the leaders I've worked with, no leader has placed as much deliberate emphasis on succession and leadership development as Ken Aldridge. It's doubtful that Ken would have done so were it not for the butt kicking he received over thirty years prior to his own succession. It became the seminal event in Ken's growth as a leader, causing him to value succession planning and leadership development as essential to running a sustainable business. His father's sudden death had humbled him with the profound knowledge that no leader lives forever, so you must constantly be preparing the next generation of leaders.

Getting to Acceptance

Embarrassment and humiliation cut deep, and no one escapes these funky feelings. Growth is painful. Consequently, a butt kick is nearly always a painful event initially. The end result, though, is that good and rewarding things can grow out of that pain. That growth is contingent upon acceptance. Here are five tips that will help you choose acceptance over rejection:

> ➤ **Answer the holy question.** Here are the four most important words in the English language: What do you want? Think of your answer in lifelong terms. What kind of person do you want to be? What kind of ideals do you want to stand for? What kind of mark do you want to leave on the world? When you see your butt kicks as events that can actually move you closer your desires, they become less threatening.
>
> ➤ **Be courageous.** Initially, your butt kick will make you feel raw and vulnerable. It takes courage to

allow yourself to feel these feelings. Courage is not found in comfort. Be courageous by embracing the discomfort your butt kick causes. Learn more about this in chapter 10.

➤ **Control what you can.** Much about a butt kick is beyond our control. We don't get to choose, for example, the timing of the kick, who kicks us, and how hard the kick is. But how we respond to the butt kick is entirely within our control. For example, after getting fired, Pete, our IT director, could have control of writing his resume, lining up job interviews, working with an executive coach to process his kick, and more. Acceptance is easier when you have some semblance, however small, of control.

➤ **Reduce judgment, increase honesty.** When your butt kick comes, don't waste time obsessing about all the ways you've let yourself down. Instead, get out a piece of paper and list all the ways you may have contributed to the kick. Be rigorously honest. Identify the lessons you'll carry forward to prevent similar kicks in the future.

➤ **Surrender.** Nearly all of life's greatest lessons come down to these two words: let go. Only by releasing your tight grip on how you wanted things to be can you fully accept things as they are. Let go of the condition that existed before the kick, so you can grab hold of the better leader you can be after the butt-kick lessons take root.

KICKASS COMEBACKS: Shindig Edition

Oh how the mighty fall. In 2003, at the height of their career, the Dixie Chicks, the best-selling female group of all time, plummeted back down to earth. Nine days before the U.S. invasion of Iraq, while performing in London, lead singer Natalie Maines told the crowd, "We don't want this war, this violence, and we're ashamed that the president of the United States [George W. Bush] is from Texas." The British audience erupted with applause.

Almost overnight, the supergroup was blackballed in the country music world, which is famously right wing. Within a week, their single "Landslide" plunged from ten to forty-three on the Hot 100 list. They lost a sponsorship deal with Lipton tea. Political pundits told them to "shut up and sing." The group received death threats.

The Dixie Chicks used the backlash as fodder for their creative energy. While exiled from country music, they wrote *Taking the Long Way*, which was released to critical acclaim in 2006. The album won seven Grammy Awards, including Album of the Year, and the single "I'm Not Ready to Make Nice" took home Record of the Year and Song of the Year. The song amounts to a refusal to apologize for their antiwar comments and remains the band's biggest U.S. single.

Source: Grady Smith, "Is Country Music Ready to Forgive the Dixie Chicks?," *Guardian*, November 19, 2015, https://www.theguardian.com/music/2015/nov/19/the-dixie-chicks-tour-is-country-music-ready-to-forgive.

Stop Being a Reject

Nothing stunts leadership growth as much as closed-mindedness. When your ability for self-reflection is shut down, personal accountability is next to impossible. Blaming others or giving excuses for our own faults, mistakes, and imperfections is an all too common butt-kick response. Rejecting feedback is more common than accepting it, and too many leaders miss out on the opportunity for personal growth just to protect the image they hold of themselves.

We expect a lot from our leaders. Most especially, we want them to be right. We want them to pursue the right goals, say the right things, make the right decisions, take the right actions, and, above all, treat us right. Maybe it's natural, then, that leaders protect themselves from looking wrong, even when fessing up would be the right choice.

It takes a very self-aware and courageous leader to say, "I was wrong" or "I messed up" or "It was my fault." Yet, saying these powerful words often endears a leader to those being led. There is something completely disarming, and even attractive, about a leader who admits when he or she is wrong. Something profoundly important is revealed and communicated when a leader admits a mistake: her humanness.

Nothing stunts leadership growth as much as closed-mindedness. When your ability for self-reflection is shut down, personal accountability is next to impossible.

PART II

Career Kicks

No leader gets to permanently avoid an ass kicking. Throughout your leadership career, and especially when your leadership gets off track, your ego will get leveled. These experiences are a sort of reset button, causing you to reconsider the leader you are and the actions you need to take to become the leader you'd like to be.

In this section you'll learn

- ➤ harsh leadership realities that nearly all new leaders face, which often result in a crisis of confidence,
- ➤ why the things that caused you to become a leader aren't the things that will make you successful as a leader,
- ➤ the meaning of the Holy Shift and why making the conversion is critical to becoming a good leader,
- ➤ common ego blows that seasoned leaders face, and productive ways for dealing with them.

You're going to face (and cause) lots of butt kicks during the course of your leadership career. This section will illustrate common kicks that leaders experience at different career stages, while providing practical tips for strengthening your leadership effectiveness regardless of which stage you're in now.

CHAPTER 3

Kick Me, I'm New!

Would I rather be feared or loved? Easy. Both. I want
people to be afraid of how much they love me.
—Michael Scott, *The Office*

For new leaders in particular, a kick in the butt is inevitable. In the same way people without children can't really know what it's like to have kids until they do, you can't really know what it's like to be a leader until you actually lead. Even organizations that invest in leadership development struggle with helping new leaders fully comprehend what it means to lead. Leadership programs often emphasize the operational mechanics of leading—planning, organizing, budgeting, or content that leans more toward management, such as delegating, time management, and giving feedback. What most leadership programs neglect to cover, but that new leaders quickly discover, is that leadership is massively freakin' hard. What is left out is how political, shifting, and unpredictable leadership is. Also absent is how much the emotional aspects of leading overshadow and often interfere with the mechanical ones. Consequently, the excitement of finally moving into a leadership role, sometimes after years of toiling among the rank and file, quickly gives way to intense feelings of pressure, anxiety, and inadequacy. After moving into their first leadership role, new leaders are often dumbstruck by how ill prepared they are for leading others.

The startling discovery that leading others is way harder than first imagined is often a leader's first kick in the ass, laying the ground work for bigger butt kicks that are sure to come. Here are just a few of the raw realities that quickly confront new leaders:

> ➤ **Adults are big babies.** You lead people, and people are fickle, quirky, and often petty. On occasion, even experienced employees will act childish, like grown-up toddlers wearing bigger clothes and sporting larger and more fragile egos. Sure, they can be smart, passionate, and upstanding too. The problem is the unpredictability. On any given day, in any given work situation, it is hard to predict which people are going to act like adults and which are going to act like whiney, sniveling, irritable babies. Some people will respond to your feedback receptively; others will get defensive or stew with resentment. And some days you'll be the biggest baby in the room—usually when you think everyone around you is acting infantile.
>
> ➤ **Demands are relentless, unforgiving bastards.** You're only deemed successful as a leader if you get results. The drive to produce results is incessant. No matter how well you do this quarter, or with this project, or with this customer, you'll be

expected to do more and better next time. Your
reputation is always on the line. The pressure is
multiplied by the fact that people are counting
on you to not let them down. Your organization
holds you to the same expectation. And when the
needs of your direct reports conflict with the needs
of the company, you'll be caught in the vise of
competing demands.

➤ **Making people uncomfortable is your job.** Leadership has everything to do with creating, managing,
and effecting change, which, by definition, is uncomfortable. People are comfort-preferring crea-
tures. That said, human beings (and organizations)
don't grow in a zone of comfort. We grow, progress, and evolve in a zone of *dis*comfort. The harsh
reality is that your job as a leader is to make people
uncomfortable. Doing otherwise breeds complacency. Thus, you have to constantly be stretching
people toward higher goals and standards. But
guess what? People generally don't appreciate you
making them uncomfortable.

➤ **The cavalry isn't coming.** Self-reliance is a hallmark
of strong leadership. You'll sometimes feel under
siege from the volume and intensity of the challenges
you're facing. Regardless, you'll be expected to
bring them to resolution—without the aid of a
handbook. Leadership can be a lonely endeavor.
With no cavalry to rescue you, you're forced to
grope your way through, often making things up
as you go along. As a result, you'll often feel like a

fake on the inside while straining to portray confidence on the outside.

➤ **The biggest problem is mostly you.** Leaders are not like everybody else. The reason that people don't put in the same obnoxious hours you do, don't view all tasks as urgent, don't click their heels and say "Yessir!" to every directive, and don't deliver twenty-four-carat quality is that they shouldn't. Neither should you. But often you do, mostly to the detriment of their results and your health. Leaders often get in their own way by being overly judgmental, holding people to unrealistic standards, and caring more for results than people. You'll be blind to all of this, of course. Your direct reports won't have the courage to tell you about your contribution to the insanity.

Faced with such startling realities, the attraction of leading that held the new leader's gaze before moving into a leadership role quickly loses its luster. At this honeymoon-is-over stage, new leaders question whether they even want to be leaders anymore. Leadership, the new leader realizes, is a messy business.

The Bigger the Delusion, the Sharper the Sting

Before moving into a leadership role, there is an innocent naïveté about what leadership will entail. The more deluded a new leader is about leadership before becoming a leader, the more badly an ass kicking stings. The starting assumption about leadership is that your ideas will be listened to, valued, and heeded. That your impact, influence, and income will grow. From afar it looks attractive, as if the practice of leadership boiled down to issuing orders, imparting wisdom, developing underlings, effecting results, and reaping rewards. It all seems pretty straightforward.

Once you become a leader, you learn that leadership is not all sunshine and lollipops. Leadership is much more about *those being led* than the person doing the leading. Leaders are successful to the extent that they help others become successful. Self-determination has very little to do with it. Leaders are almost entirely dependent on the output, performance, and growth of the people they're leading. Leaders need followers more than followers need leaders. Followers make leaders successful. The core truth obscured by the delusion that leadership is about the leader is that, to excel, a leader can only do well by helping others do well. Unless the leader focuses intensely on building up the capability and successes of others, his or her leadership potential will never be fully realized. The people whom the leader is leading are the whole point of leadership.

After getting psychologically kicked by the hard realities of leading others, new leaders may seriously question their competence and sanity. *This isn't what I signed up for*, they may think. *Why suffer through all this one-upmanship, second-guessing, poor attitudes, and political nonsense?* During my leadership development programs, I have new leaders answer this simple question: At the end of your leadership career, what will have made the challenge of leadership all worthwhile? By far the most frequent answer goes something like this: "I will have built other leaders who themselves are building other leaders."

When you are privileged to lead others, your influence can impact the trajectories of people's entire careers, potentially helping them become more courageous, just, and humane. When you do it right, the best of you may bring out the best in others. In the process, they may become inspired to lead too. The pain associated with enduring the hardships of leading others is offset by the satisfaction of making a positive difference for the people and organization you serve.

Once you become a leader, you learn that leadership is not all sunshine and lollipops.

The starting point of effective leadership development (and true leadership change) is the recognition that leadership is ridiculously freakin' hard. Starting with this presumption helps mitigate overconfidence, inspire earnest preparation, and activate a deeper and more authentic commitment to lead. Ultimately, by soberly and thoughtfully assessing how crazy hard leadership is, you'll stop freaking out about having to lead. Leadership is not just hard for you; it's hard, period. You want to lead? Deal with it.

Sorry, Hercules, You Can't Do It Alone

Before you become responsible for direct reports, your success is largely self-determined. You solve you own problems, perform your own tasks, and can draw a direct connection between your work ethic and your productivity. But once you move into a leadership role and take on the added responsibility (and burden) of direct reports, everything changes. Problems become multidimensional, work gets done through other people, and the connection between your leadership work ethic and the output of your team becomes more indirect. It takes a while to learn that the more work you personally take on, the less productive the team becomes. Early on, the temptation is to equate your personal productivity with the effectiveness of your team, so you start grabbing hold of tasks that are better left to them. You add their work to your work. After all, it was personal productivity that made you successful before you moved into the leadership role. Self-performing and overworking were strategies that made you successful before, you figure, so loading up on more tasks can only help you succeed, right? It's an impossible feat, of course, and you quickly get subsumed by attempting to know and do everyone else's job.

The DIY Leader

"Get 'er done" is a common refrain in the construction business, and often said with pride by Michael, the heir apparent of a $500 million highway-building company in the Midwest. The company bears his last name, and Michael literally grew up in the business, starting out by sweeping floors in the equipment department. After college and a few summer internships, he immediately moved into a leadership role in the company. His path is similar to that of many children within family-owned businesses where birthright trumps merit. The son or daughter of the owner rockets right past many more qualified and seasoned nonfamily personnel to take a leadership role that he or she is handed without earning or deserving it. In some respects, the pressure to show people that they will do a great job for the company and everyone in it only intensifies the situation. They try to "earn" the role *after* moving into it, by overworking, overtrying, and overmanaging. Michael did too. He felt that he needed to know as much about every piece of the business as fast as humanly possible.

Michael's grandfather had been dirt poor and had built the business from the ground up. Michael's father had helped expand the business a hundredfold. Michael's very identity and worth would be, in his eyes, judged against how much the company expanded under his watch. Michael's response to his high-stakes situation was to spend obnoxious hours at work, rarely taking a day off. His daytime hours were spent at the jobsite, micromanaging his field laborers. His evening hours were spent reviewing financial and production reports that he could scarcely comprehend. To the words "Get 'er done," Michael had added, "yourself." His social life was dead. What had once seemed like a fantastic opportunity—to become the company's standard-bearer—was turning out to be a cold slap in the face. Only a birdbrain would want a life like this, he thought.

Sure, quitting was an option. But if Michael were to quit, imagine the burden he would carry for the rest of his life. He'd become the big family letdown. He would somehow be lesser than his father and grandfather. If he quit, it would prove that they had more grit, guts, and gall. For them to have succeeded in the business, and for him to have quit, would have meant that they had bigger cojones than he did. He would, in short, be less of a man, undeserving of his family name.

Michael didn't quit. It just wasn't in his DNA. Instead, his leadership coaching focused on slowing down his pace and shifting his focus. It started by doing a "day in the life" exercise whereby he envisioned a day in his life three years hence, when he was thriving as a leader and living a life that he would want to live. By clarifying the life he wanted, he could start navigating away from his early leadership missteps. He wanted to delegate more so he wouldn't have to manage every detail of his team's work. He wanted to understand those stupid reports so he could review them quicker. He wanted to be free from the burden of feeling like he had to work so many godforsaken hours. He wanted to *enjoy* being a leader and the opportunity to steward the company during his time with the business.

Once he defined what he wanted and didn't want, he came to the recognition that trying to learn everything all at once was futile and counterproductive. His dad was right when he told him to view his career as a marathon, not a sprint. Instead of trying to know everything himself, he began tapping into the experience and mentorship of the people who were more seasoned than him, which, it turned out, came with the added benefit of building relationships with them. By engaging them in his growth and development, he involved them more in his career. They had a genuine vested interest in helping him succeed. Knowing that gave him more confidence.

KICKASS COMEBACKS: Soldier Edition

In 1521, Íñigo López de Loyola suffered severe injuries in the Battle of Pamplona after a cannonball shattered his leg. Íñigo was no ordinary warrior; he was a Spanish knight from an esteemed Basque family who had joined the army at seventeen. He dueled fiercely, killing many foes. He had demonstrated so much battlefield courage that, out of respect, his French enemies carried him all the way back from the battlefield to his hometown of Loyola.

During his convalescence Íñigo grew bored and frustrated. He was a warrior, after all, meant to be on the battlefield. As a wounded warrior, Íñigo was humiliated and depressed. He settled on passing his time by reading the only text available on his nightstand: a book about the life of saints.

To say that Íñigo was transfixed by what he read would be an understatement. He began having spiritual visions, ultimately causing him to give up being a soldier and dedicate himself to living a monastic life. He laid his military garments in front of an image of the Virgin Mary during a pilgrimage to Montserrat, the Benedictine monastery in the mountains of Spain. Then he traveled to Manresa in Catalonia, and spent months living alone in a cave. There, he developed a series of spiritual exercises centered on silence and contemplation.

If not for a cannonball and the wounding of a soldier, the Jesuit order of the Catholic Church would not exist. Íñigo López de Loyola is now known as Saint Ignatius of Loyola, the founder of the Society of Jesus, better known as the Jesuit order. The Jesuits are widely respected as being more intellectually open than other Catholic orders, and many renowned institutions of higher learning (including Georgetown, Fordham, Marquette, Gonzaga, and Boston College) are led by the Jesuits.

Jesuits are sometimes referred to as "God's Soldiers," reflecting the conversion of Ignatius from a mortal to a spiritual warrior.

After Ignatius, the second most famous Jesuit is Jorge Mario Bergoglio, now known as Pope Francis.

Sources: "St. Ignatius Loyola," New Advent Catholic Encyclopedia, http://www .newadvent.org/cathen/07639c.htm; George Traub and Debra Mooney, "A Biography of St. Ignatius Loyola: The Founder of the Jesuits," Xavier University website, http://www.xavier.edu/mission-identity/heritage-tradition/who-was-St-Ignatius -Loyola.cfm.

Holy Shift

The shift that a kick in the ass of a new leader can effect is from sel*fish*ness to sel*fless*ness. Instead of thinking, *How successful can I be?*, the thinking shifts to *What can I do to help* them *be more successful?* Instead of treating people as resources who do work for you, you shift to being a resource for them. You begin collaborating with them to set goals. You remove barriers to their performance. You provide skill-stretching assignments and training opportunities. You give them air cover when pressure comes down from above. Instead of acting as a cop who enforces rules, watches for violations, and punishes noncompliance, you become a coach who invests time in their development, draws out a higher level of performance, and helps them take pride in their work. A good butt kick for a new leader should startle him out of any rosy leadership delusions and help him evolve past being interested in himself to being much more interested in the people he is fortunate to lead.

The idea is for you, as a leader, to serve those you're leading by putting your leadership influence to work for them. By "serve" I don't mean like a white-gloved butler who is careful not to disturb people as he adjusts their lobster bibs. I mean taking intentional, deliberate, and assertive *action* for the good of others. Success as a leader is contingent on bettering the lives and careers of the people you are leading. Leadership, in other words, is not about you; it's about them. Getting over yourself is a must. The less focused on yourself you are, the better you'll get as a leader. That's true for leaders of any age.

Butt kicks teach new leaders that the fastest way to great results is taking a genuine and active interest in helping others succeed. When you focus on using your leadership for the good of others, you take a genuine interest in getting to know their needs, goals, aspirations, and gifts. You start helping people build skills, confidence, and self-reliance so they can add more value to the company and their careers. When the Holy Shift has truly taken hold, you become an aggressive champion, builder, and developer of others.

A Leader Who Has Made the Holy Shift

- Embodies his or her values
- Is self-aware, conscious of his or her *sunshine* and *shadows*
- Is keenly observant and listens deeply
- Has a strong desire to help others win
- Shares war stories and shows battle scars
- Is confident and humble, and in the right proportions
- Knows that his or her success is based on bringing out the leader in others
- Is nontoxic and treats people respectfully

Butt-Kicking Tips for New Leaders

One of the main points of this book is that butt kicks are good because they can startle you out of focusing on yourself and get you focused on others. So, new leaders, consider these tips mini butt kicks to take in good stride!

➤ **Get over yourself.** At this stage in your leadership career, you don't have enough of a track record to be bragging so much. Stop trying to prove to everyone how smart, competent, or in command you are. Fixating on the rung above you—and the bigger salary you assume it comes with—just shows others that you're self-centered. Try this instead: focus on helping your direct reports get promoted.

➤ **Shut your piehole.** You don't know squat. So stop commenting or giving critiques after other people share ideas. Monitor your talking-to-listening ratio. Then listen a lot more than you talk. If you pay attention to how the most experienced leaders carry themselves, you'll see that biting one's tongue is a hallmark of seasoned judgment.

➤ **Stop bellyaching.** It's common for new leaders to be excessively hard on themselves, which makes them too negative. Practice gratitude. At the start of each day, list at least three things for which you are grateful. Tell people that you're grateful for their contributions. The more thankful you are, the more positive you'll be for others.

➤ **Don't be a slob.** Nothing says "I'm a crappy leader" as much as being a disorganized slob. Stop building skyscrapers with the stacks of paper on your desk.

Show some self-respect and clean up your work-space. Take an interest in dressing better, eating better, and taking better care of yourself. Be better.

> **Stun your tech.** Put down your stupid smartphone and actually talk to people. 'Nuff said.

> **Get to work.** Just because you're in a leadership role doesn't mean you're a leader. Becoming a good and effective leader takes hard work. Go someplace away from the office, where you can actually get some work done, and write your answers to these questions:

- Why do you want to lead?
- What do you already *think* you know about leading? How were those beliefs and opinions formed?
- Among the leaders you've been led by, which ones do you admire? What makes them so admirable? What qualities do they have that you'd like to develop?
- What contribution do you want to make to your organization by applying your leadership? What talents will you need to strengthen or develop in order to make that contribution?
- What contribution do you want to make to your neighborhood, community, and the world through your leadership?
- What positive difference do you want to make in the lives of the people you're fortunate to lead?

CHAPTER 4

The Cheeky Middle

Life is like a dogsled team. If you ain't the
lead dog, the scenery never changes.

—Lewis Grizzard

A h, the middle place. This is the point in your leader-ship career where nothing is certain, and everything is up for grabs. It's like being in the middle of an ocean: you're far from where you launched and still a long way from the safe shores. As a leader, your development is well under way, but nowhere near complete; you are formed but not finished.

Much of what makes midcareer so challenging is that everyone wants a piece of you. Your employees want your time, guidance, and recognition. Your bosses want your loyalty, diligence, and competence. Both groups want your leadership, but each toward different aims. Your employees want your leadership devoted to giving them opportunities to grow and excel. For them, your influence as a leader should be aimed at making their jobs more fulfilling, stable, and secure. How you treat them—emotionally, developmentally, and financially—will have a direct impact on how hard they work, and how loyal they are to you and the organization. It's in your best interest to meet their needs. After all, where would you be as a leader without their hard work and loyalty?

Your bosses' needs are different. First, it's important to be clear about what they don't want: surprises. Nothing will get your boss more steamed than bringing her a problem well after the time she actually could have helped resolve it. Handing her the ticking problem precisely at the time when it is set to explode is the surest way to damage your relationship with your boss and, it follows, your career. Advancement as a midcareer leader requires minimizing, mitigating, and controlling risk. When it comes to pleasing the people above you, heed these words: no surprises!

What else do your bosses want? Results. How you care for your employees, generally, means less to them than how you care for the organization and its goals. If taking care of your employees furthers the organization's aims, have at it. But if doing so slows down progress or harms results, they'd prefer that you direct your attention elsewhere. It's hard to argue with their logic; without sustainable results, people don't have jobs. You want to care for your people? You want them to have stable jobs? You want to help them make more money? Put getting results first.

Between Front and Rear

For midcareer leaders, the tension you're caught between is not just between differing wants; it's between means and ends. If you expect to continue to advance and move into the senior ranks, you had better make results happen. At the same time, motivating your people to be productive so they contribute to getting those results means treating them well and fairly. Your employees generate the results your bosses expect you to produce. Yes, organizations don't exist without results. But you need people to effect results. As a leader, you need to treat people well (means) so they get the job done (results).

When you're a leader in this middle place, you can understand both worlds. You're not so far removed from the nonleader ranks that you don't remember how demotivating it is to work for bosses who always want more and are perpetually unsatisfied. Yet you also get where your bosses are coming from. They're privy to a lot more information that people at lower levels don't see. Their outlook telescopes well beyond today's minutia, and includes all the incoming threats that, sometimes, jeopardize the organization's survival. The drive for results is incessant because, they believe, the organization's very existence depends on it. At this stage in your leadership, you're starting to believe it too.

The challenge for midcareer leaders is to balance the means-and-ends tension created by the differing wants of your direct reports and bosses. Sure, you'll have to occasionally take sides, but much more regularly you have to be on both sides. You have to get results *and* you have to treat people well. Generally, you get the results (ends) through the means (treatment of people). If, as a midcareer leader, you favor one over the other, the organization or the people will suffer. So will your effectiveness as a leader.

Notice, by the way, the very necessity of the means/ends tension itself. If people stopped expecting good treatment, what would prevent leaders from mistreating them? Conversely, if there were no drive to get results, work itself would flatline into boredom, and apathy would reign. The tension is healthy for the organization and its people.

If You Jilt Them, They Will Kick

Advancing as a midcareer leader requires attending to the needs of your bosses and direct reports. Ass kicks come when either group feels jilted. If, for example, your direct reports sense that all you care about is getting results, and that they are little more than "resources" pointed only toward that end, they will become convinced that you don't care about them. When that happens, they'll stop being loyal to you, and without their loyalty, your career can become unmoored.

Consider, for instance, Gus, the communications director of a large professional services company. Given his role, Gus feels that he has to "be in the know," so he gets himself invited to as many senior executive meetings as he possibly can. It's his way of staying in the communication flow, so he can discern which information needs to be shared and which must be concealed from the rank and file. You could think of him as a propagandist, advancing his leaders' agenda by communicating no more than they want to have communicated. Pinpointing what to communicate, and what not to, requires Gus to have close relationships with each of the company's business unit leaders, which includes his own boss. Gus prides himself on the relationships he has developed. On occasion, he has even been known to take an extended lunch so he could walk his boss's dog.

Gus's team, unbeknownst to his bosses, thinks he's a fake and a suck-up. He's the head of communications, but has never written one company memo, newsletter article, or press release. Instead of doing real work, like them, all he does is talk all day, in the executive meetings where he lives. He's in so many of them that he's almost entirely unreachable. When his team members try to reach him, their messages always get diverted straight to voicemail, which is often full. Compounding his team's feelings of neglect is the fact that no one on Gus's team has had their yearly performance review, despite having been directed by Gus to announce the annual review process to the entire workforce months ago.

Gus's team members scratch their heads, perplexed at how such seemingly smart people as the company leaders could be so snookered by an imposter like Gus. But Gus's leaders are happy because the communication apparatus is working. Not only are the messages they want relayed getting sent, but Gus speaks their lingo, reciting such business-speak as, "We need to be mindful of the value-add for the consumer so we can capture more of their share of wallet." Gus, his bosses are convinced, "gets it." Gus, too, thinks his career is going well. He's pleasing his bosses, and that's what matters, right?

Ask yourself, can Gus really be successful in the long term if his attention is only pointed in one direction? Can he really advance without the loyalty of his team? Of course not. Gus is a real person (though I changed his name), and the butt kick he eventually got was a direct result of losing his team's loyalty. First, a team member quit, citing Gus's poor leadership in her exit interview. Then one of Gus's team members complained to one of the business unit leaders about Gus never being around, and being delinquent on the yearly performance reviews. Finally, Gus lost the favor of his own boss. Her boss had chided her for letting Gus take long lunches to walk her dog. Without the loyalty of his team or his boss, the ice under Gus's job security became thin. Eventually, as you might have guessed, the company "freed him up to his future."

Notice the boomerang effect: Gus showed no loyalty to his team, so they withdrew their loyalty from him. Without that, his career was doomed.

Automatic for the People

Whereas ignoring the needs of your people will harm your career, overattending to them is equally harmful. Some midcareer leaders take particular pride in providing "air cover" for their department, protecting them from incoming demands and changes. While this is, indeed, an important function of a leader, some leaders go too far, acting like martyrs when they perceive directives from on high as negatively impacting the workload of their department. When changes come down, instead of considering the best interests of the enterprise as a whole, they fixate on how the changes will impact their sliver of the organization. Though they are members of the executive body, they automatically "side" with their direct reports, causing more-senior leaders to doubt whether they can make decisions objectively and in a way that balances the goals of the organization and the needs of the people. After a while, despite building tremendous loyalty with their direct reports, these midcareer martyrs may be viewed as disloyal to the organization. Even if they get great results—which they often do because of how well they treat their team—they'll get stigmatized as not being loyal enough to the company to be considered for the senior executive ranks.

I've coached a few midcareer leaders who harbored deep resentments toward their organization because, in spite of building a strong team and getting stellar results, they were excluded from the senior executive levels. "What else do I need to do?" they often ask. "My team loves me and we're getting great results. But instead of getting promoted, I'm stuck. It feels like I'm being punished for doing a great job."

You'll rarely be invited to join the senior executive ranks if your loyalty is imbalanced toward your direct re ports. Advancement requires being mutually loyal to the broader organization and to the people whom you're leading. At the senior level, decisions that are in the best interest of the organization sometimes conflict with the needs of certain people or departments. When revenues or funds are low, sometimes you have to cut costs, and often that means firing people. Investing in new products or markets sometimes means reducing the money spent in other areas, and that, too, can mean firing people. Implementing a new, sophisticated computer system may make some people's jobs irrelevant, and that can mean firing people (or at least reassigning them). In other words, certain tough calls that senior leaders make to improve the health of the organization may require kicking some people right out the door, as harsh as it may be. Being able to occasionally make these kicks, as a midcareer leader, is often the initiation by which you demonstrate that you're fit to become a senior leader.

Whereas ignoring the needs of your people
will harm your career, overattending
to them is equally harmful.

Common Midcareer Kicks

While most midcareer kicks stem from not paying enough attention to results (the "ends") or the treatment of people (the "means"), there are additional kicks that you may experience midway through your leadership career. We'll end this chapter by exploring a few of the more common midcareer kicks.

The Passover

Imagine that you're a division manager and you aspire to become the division's vice president. For the last two years you've been part of a "next level" leadership program, designed, by definition, to help you advance upward in the company. The program was launched because the company's senior leaders wanted to be thoughtful about succession planning and deepen the company's bench strength. Only the company's most promising leaders get selected to attend.

What happens next? You get promoted, right? Nope. Moving from the middle ranks to the upper ranks takes more than getting great results, treating your people well, or being tapped for the company's elite leadership program: it takes opportunity. If the company doesn't have additional upper-level positions to offer you, you won't advance. Worse yet, sometimes, almost magically, a new position opens up only to be staffed by an outsider. Yes, an outsider!

Getting passed over by an outsider actually happens a lot to midcareer leaders. If it happens to you, you may be tempted to quit. "How dare they!" you'll exclaim. "What two-faced hypocrites! They promised that I'd move up. I've busted my ass here for fifteen years, yet they go and hire some blooming outsider who knows nothing about this place! Rumor has it that the outsider is getting a fat paycheck and signing bonus too. Screw this place! I'm gonna hightail it outta here just as soon as I can!"

Not so fast, pal. If you play your cards right, someday you'll be in the room where the tough calls are made. You'll learn that when the senior leaders chose an outsider over you, it's not because they were intentionally plotting to hold back your career. In many instances, the outsider comes with an expertise or capability that the organization is trying to develop. In other instances, the outsider has access to a market that the organization is trying to strike into. The outsider comes to the company with unique knowledge about the market or with a preexisting book of business—instantly justifying their salary and worth. So what magically appeared as a new position was really just a calculated and opportunistic decision by the senior executives. Instantly gaining new capabilities, or being able to gain entry into a new market by hiring outside expertise, can be a great strategy for organizational growth.

Sure, it can be frustrating staring upward while your bosses add to the number of seats above you and then fill them with the butts of outsiders. Sometimes it feels like your advancement is forever bumping up against an "ass ceiling." But complaining will just make you look like a baby, which is wholly unbecoming of a leader. There are better and more leader-like approaches, including:

➤ **Bring the outsider in.** Help the new person be successful. If he or she is as good as the company thinks, they'll value you when you show them the ropes and help them navigate the company's political realities.

➤ **Trust your leaders.** Other than hiring the outsider, has the company generally had your back? Give them the benefit of the doubt. If they tell you that your future is still bright, and that opportunities are bound to emerge, believe them. Then ask them what you can do to help create additional opportunities that you might be able to fulfill.

➤ **Grab the ring yourself.** The more your results are unassailable and the deeper the loyalty you have among your people, the closer you'll be to stepping onto the next rung. The division manager of a drilling company, for example, helped develop so much business (doubling its size in three years) and had developed such goodwill among his people that when his boss, a VP, retired, the company didn't even bother recruiting external candidates. The DM had earned it and deserved it.

What's worse than getting passed over by an outsider? Getting passed over by a peer! Boom! It can be especially painful gearing yourself up for the next ladder rung only to be bypassed by the person you work beside. Even people who seem astonishingly less qualified than you can sometimes speed right by you, smiling and waving as they do. Again, complaining won't do much good. Stick to the same approach that you use when getting bypassed by an experienced outsider: help them be successful, trust your bosses, and start getting clear and unassailable results.

The Smackdown

In the early stages of your leadership career, which we covered in the last chapter, you will make a lot of mistakes. But those mistakes, in relative terms, are generally not all that consequential, and most can be dismissed as "rookie mistakes." In midcareer, though, leadership mistakes can have a broader impact and aren't as easily dismissed.

In the middle of your leadership career, you're likely to experience your first big failure. Often, the failure will cost the organization you work for a lot of money. In the worst instances, your failure may bring reputational damage to the organization. Even if you can line up plenty of excuses for why the failure happened, it won't matter; it is still *your* failure. Regardless of whether you keep your job, it will rattle your confidence to the core.

The stronger your track record of performance before the failure, the more it will knock you off guard. A senior project manager at one of my construction company clients, for example, had led project after project successfully. As his confidence grew, so did the confidence his senior leaders had in his ability. When the company landed a big new job with a big new client in a big new market, they tapped him because he was tried and true. Despite his track record and the sound reasoning of his bosses, he failed miserably, costing the company millions of dollars.

It's not surprising that the project failed. It was a client the company had never worked with before in a market where it had no experience. The senior project manager, though, internalized the failure as his own. Believing that it was the honorable thing to do, he submitted his resignation to his boss, the division VP.

Failure, for high achievers such as those with a leadership profile, can be crushing. Emotions of fear, insecurity, and doubt can rent space in your mind for months afterward. Where you once were bold and sure, now you're tentative and hesitant. The ambition and confidence that had, until now, defined your success, recedes. Maybe, you start to think, you're not a leader after all. Or, if you are, you're a bad one.

At this point, an ass kicking from a wise and more senior person can be helpful. The division VP had enough gray hairs to realize that a host of factors had contributed to the project failure, and that the senior project manager had done as well as anyone could have expected. Having had a few good failures during his own career gave the VP perspective. So what did he do? He rejected the resignation. More boldly, when the company won an even bigger project six months later, he staffed the same senior project manager—who now had something to prove. Seasoned with the ingrained lessons from the failure, he led the project successfully, resetting his career in the process. Below are some tips that midcareer leaders can use if they experience a big failure:

➤ **Sulk.** Look, you're going to sulk, so I won't patron-
ize you by telling you not to. That said, make your
sulking productive. Carve out time to be alone. Go
sit by a lake, go for a long drive, or tap into your
inner Forrest Gump and go for a long, long run.
Whatever you do, though, don't sulk around other
people. Being around a sulker ain't fun!

➤ **Get perspective.** Yes, you're embarrassed, and you
feel that you've just convinced your senior leaders
that you don't have what it takes to be one of them.
In fact, nearly all of them likely experienced a big
career failure. Find one who has, tell her what
you're going through, and tap into her wisdom.

➤ **Process the lessons.** Think of your failure as a
degree from an elite university where you got
"schooled." Your failure is a grueling type of education. You wouldn't want to go through it again,
but the lessons you learned are invaluable and will
have a positive and enduring impact on your
career. It's a good idea for you to document all
the lessons you learned so you can quickly refer
to them when facing similar challenges in the
future. That way you won't have to repeat any
classes!

The Ebbing

At some point at this middle stage of your leadership
career, it's common to be consumed with a gnawing sense
that "there must be something more." The job of a leader,
which looked so enviable when you were younger and at
lower levels, feels less satisfying than you had imagined.

The headaches are frequent, the pressures are unrelenting, and the rewards less satisfying than you had hoped. Worse, everyone is depending on you: your bosses, your employees, your clients, and your family. You're spread so thin that, when it comes to your attention, everyone seems to get a little gypped—including yourself.

Something else may nag you at this stage, something more troublesome. You feel like you're selling small portions of your soul each day. You find yourself making decisions at work that go against the principles you hold outside work. With each small compromise of your principles, you feel like your work self and your "real" self are becoming increasingly disconnected. You're becoming someone you never thought you would be: a sellout. You worry that you're selling your soul, but you're not sure who the buyer is.

I call this midcareer leadership stage "Ebbing." Not every leader experiences this distinct low point, but those who do fear that it extends indefinitely. *What if this is all there is?* they worry. *What if becoming a more senior leader just brings more headaches, more pressure, more compromises, more ass kissing, and less fulfillment? How much of my soul am I willing to sell?*

Ebbing is a time of reflection and reassessment when you'll have more questions than answers. The questions you grapple with during the Ebbing stage are well worth answering because they will influence the kind of leader you will ultimately be. If you find yourself deep in the ebb, pay close attention to the questions that surface for you. Recognize that, eventually, the tide will roll back in, and the decisions you make during the ebb may end up defining the extent to which your leadership makes a positive difference in the lives of those whom your leadership will touch. The resolutions you make while ebbing will influence how grounded you'll be if you acquire more leadership stature and power.

Here are some questions for the ebbing leader to consider:

- ➤ Who do I aim to be as a leader?
- ➤ What true difference do I hope to make through my leadership?
- ➤ How do I wish to treat people while I'm leading? How do I wish to be treated as a leader?
- ➤ What principles will I uphold? What compromises am I unwilling to make?
- ➤ What actions do I need to take to close the gap between the leader I aim to be and the leader I am today?
- ➤ Can I become the leader I want to become by working where I work today?

Kicks in the middle of your leadership career cut deeper than when you first became a leader. Getting passed over or smacked down are experiences you don't want to relive. Likewise, when your enthusiasm for leading ebbs, you'll call into question everything associated with your current and future identity as a leader. The cheeky middle, in other words, is a supremely important place. Rather than endure it, embrace it as an essential part of your leadership development. Do that, and you'll benefit from what you learn when you become a senior leader—the focus of the next chapter.

CHAPTER 5

Shrinking Big Shots
Seasoned Leaders Getting Their Kicks

The older you get, the stronger the wind gets—
and it's always in your face.
—Pablo Picasso

Even grizzled workplace veterans contend with getting their butts kicked. For seasoned leaders, a butt kick often comes with the shrinking of your importance or the diminishing of everything you've already accomplished.

Imagine building a long and positive track record as a leader. You've earned your stripes through hard work, persistence, and dedication. You've suffered through, and learned from, many butt kicks. You've given more to the organization than it has given to you. Most importantly, you've made the Holy Shift, making a real, positive, and enduring difference in the lives of those you've led. The organization and the people you've led are better off because of your contributions. You are at the top of your game.

What comes on the other side of all that success? *Cresting*. One day you will walk into work and things will be ever so slightly different. Your energy will be just a smidge lower. You will barely be able to notice that you are a tad less concerned about the things that, up until now, got you hot under the collar. People's problems will seem just a little less significant, and your response when they bring them to you will register with a hint of dispassion. These changes will be barely noticeable at first. But after teetering over the summit of your leadership game, every successive day thereafter will be stretched out over a long, slow decline. Like a reflection of life itself, nobody leads forever.

Cresting, that inevitable condition where the best days of your leadership career are no longer in front of you, brings feelings of increasingly uncomfortable contentment. Simply put, you care a little less than you used to. Sure, you're still *in* the game, you're just not at the top of it. You still attend the important meetings, you still get a speaking slot at the annual business offsite, and people still seek out your input before making big changes. But your luster is less lustrous. The full weight of your influence has become lighter.

For seasoned leaders, a butt kick often comes with the shrinking of your importance or the diminishing of everything you've already accomplished.

One cold reality on the backside of the crest is that you will never have a leadership role of the same significance as the one you hold now. This is it. There is no larger mountain to climb. Having something to prove is hugely motivating for your career because it stiffens your sense of purpose. At the later stage of your leadership career, though, you've already proven yourself. The ambition it once took to make your mark and establish your worth is less necessary. In between mustered-up spikes in enthusiasm, there's a more general lack of excitement. Cresting comes with a loss of belly-fire that only a been-there-done-that seasoned leader can fully comprehend. At the tail end of your leadership career, purpose may give way to listlessness.

Torschlusspanik: Fear of Closing Gates

Leaders get jazzed by creating opportunities to grow and develop people and organizations. Much of the excitement of leadership comes from the opportunities that leaders are able to identify, shape, and exploit. In a very real way, leaders are opportunity creators.

One of my previous books, *Leaders Open Doors*, highlights the central leadership responsibility of opening doors of opportunity for others. There is something completely energizing and gratifying about using your influence for the good of others. For this reason, leaders are constantly on the lookout for skill-stretching, spirit-stirring, and standard-raising opportunities—for the people they lead, and for themselves.

What makes cresting so challenging for the seasoned leader is that there are fewer doors of opportunity to charge through. The fewer opportunities there are, the more uncomfortable the leader gets. The leader may feel acutely fearful or panicked. *Time is running out!* he may think. *There were so many other things I'd hoped to accomplish, but I'm not going to be able to get them all done!*

So common is this phenomenon that there's even a term for it: *Torschlusspanik*. The word first appeared in the Middle Ages and is literally translated as "gate-closing panic." In medieval times, when many European cities were enclosed fortresses, city residents would need to get back through the city gates by nightfall or risk getting locked out. The consequences of not getting through the gate on time could be serious, such as freezing to death, getting attacked by marauding thieves, or being eaten by wild animals!

As it relates to leadership, *Torschlusspanik* has an added dimension of melancholy, brought on by a pronounced fear of missing out. Soon the leader will be left outside the organization's gates, part of its history but exiled from its future. All of the leader's wonderful accomplishments pale in comparison to the infinite number of opportunities he or she will not experience.

So, yes, leaders open doors, but when the opportunities to do so start to close, they will feel less useful or important. Life is more vibrant and fulfilling inside the city walls than it is when you're left outside as the sun is setting.

"Special Projects": A Kick into Retirement

The fear that *Torschlusspanik* provokes can be so powerful that many senior leaders hang on too long, careful to not step outside the city gates. So much of their identity is tied up in the organization, they fear they'll have no identity when the gate closes on their career. So they become hangers-on, unable to retire but not fully contributing either. Often they'll claim that they intend to retire "in two years"—even if they first said this six years ago!

An organization will have much less tolerance for, and loyalty to, a young leader who isn't carrying his weight. For an aging leader, though, there is too much goodwill built up over time. The longer a leader has been with the company, the more love may surround her, making it harder for the company to let her go, even if she doesn't add the same value that she used to. Instead, the organization will use less direct approaches. For example, one common butt kick that companies use to ease an aging exec out the door is to take away her direct reports and assign her to a "special project" role. The move is typically couched in such a way that you don't realize that you've been sent out to pasture until you are far afield from the responsibilities you used to have. You'll be told, "The company really values your expertise and wisdom, so we'd like you to lead up our new such-and-such project because it's super important to our future . . . blah, blah, blah." In truth, a "special project" move is often the company's way of exiting you without having to fire you. The butt kick happens in slow motion. Eventually you find yourself counting paperclips just to pass the time. Once you realize that you have no power, influence, or resources, retirement becomes an attractive option.

Remember, butt kicks are mostly good things. Sometimes the company is doing for the aging leader what she didn't have the courage to do for herself. Crossing over the threshold into retirement sometimes requires a little shove from the company.

Meet Your New Boss, Mr. Pipsqueak

Another common butt kick tenured leaders experience is being reassigned to a boss who is younger and less experienced. For instance, one company long-timer was shocked to learn that he no longer reported directly to the president and had been reassigned to a rookie department director. Worse still, nobody had bothered to tell him of the shift for over a month. He discovered the move when one of his buddies started ribbing him about it. His buddy had seen it on a draft org chart. The longtime leader's title had been quietly changed from director to deputy director. People with titles always claim that titles aren't important—that is, of course, until their own gets messed with. For days after the discovery, the leader stewed with rage. "What have I done to deserve this?" he fumed. If the company wanted to demote him, why didn't they have the guts to tell him to his face?

Finally, at the end of the week, he stormed into the president's office and told him that he had invested too much in the company, and had contributed to too many of the company's successes, to ever work for anyone below the president. Either he reported to the president and remained a director, or he was outta here. Rarely do butt-kick reversals occur, but, surprisingly, in this case, it did. He would still report to the president. Wisely, the president could see that the title semantics and reporting changes meant a lot more to the exec than they did to the company. Plus, the longtime leader had been a true friend to him and the company; he loved the guy.

Most seasoned leaders who get butt kicked by being reassigned to a younger and less experienced boss aren't so lucky. Instead, they are forced to endure stupid questions, listen to rehashed ideas that have already been tried or that failed, and witness youthful brownnosing by ambitious up-and-comers. At least that's the perspective reassigned long-in-the-tooth leaders can have when working for a green-bean newbie!

The Ambassadors

The marginalization of aging leaders stings because, as mentioned, it diminishes their contributions and value. This is true regardless of where the exec sits in the pecking order, but is particularly true (and painful) the more senior the leader is. In an effort to make room for younger aspiring execs, one company reduced the scope of a number of senior executives while commensurately increasing the scope of the newer execs. A few veteran leaders were vice presidents who had been running large divisions. Though they retained their titles, the bulk of their responsibilities and decision authority got shifted to the less experienced leaders. The shift ended up making the VPs feel like senior executive eunuchs—all title and no importance.

Understandably, they viewed the shift as a big kick in the ass and started grumbling loudly. Before long, the owner of the company got wind that they were mighty miffed. He understood their plight; he had just turned sixty and, despite being the company owner, had also started feeling less needed, valued, and important. He too was feeling marginalized. He didn't want things to erode, especially since the company had set an ambitious growth goal of doubling revenues within the next five years. The company—and its next generation of leaders—needed the seasoned wisdom and perspective that only longevity provides. He worried about his aging execs becoming like those grumpy geezers you see at your local diner, constantly complaining about the young whippersnappers who were doing things the wrong way, *dagnabbit!*

The owner, to assuage the butt kick, did something truly unique and special—something that might not have been imaginable were it not for his own feelings of diminishment. He established a company Ambassador Program, consisting of execs who are over sixty years old. The ambassadors would meet monthly to apply their wisdom to current company challenges while reminiscing about how similar challenges had been faced and dealt with in the past. They created a logo, reminiscent of the superhero Avengers logo, which they wore on their shirts so that people would be able to identify them, and thus approach them with problems to be solved. They set a mission of providing direction, support, and corporate memory to the company. The company also reinvigorated the seasoned executives by having them

> ➤ establish a "life plan" so the company could better understand the contribution that each wanted to continue to make to the company, as well as help each exec forecast the eventual transition away from the company,
> ➤ help assimilate new executives into the company culture when they were hired from the outside,
> ➤ coteach the company's leadership and training workshops,
> ➤ mentor newly promoted executives,
> ➤ conduct safety audits, quality inspections, and jobsite visits.

The launching of the Ambassador Program, led by the company owner, sent a message to the entire workforce that company longevity is valued and wanted. It showed the older executives, in a tangible way, that their contributions were still needed. Experience matters, and drawing on the experiences of the company's senior executives would help the company to hit its growth goals and create an enduring future. They became important again.

Then Again . . .

The transition of a leader's career from the top of the crest to the other side can actually be a beautiful thing. This is the time when your wisdom is ripest, when the bulk of your legacy has been established, and when your influence has left a tangible and positive mark. At this stage of your leadership career, you are a leader in full. It's worth noting that the leadership influence of many leaders became fully expressed late in life. Benjamin Franklin was seventy when he signed the Declaration of Independence (Samuel Whittemore was eighty-one). Ronald Reagan was sixty-nine when he became president, and seventy-seven when he left office. Golda Meir became prime minister of Israel when she was seventy-one. Dr. Ray Irani, the CEO of Occidental Petroleum, is currently seventy-five years old, making him the oldest Fortune 500 CEO.

While your leadership career may span many years, the current average retirement age in the United States is sixty-two. Given that average life expectancies have been steadily growing, figuring out what to do with all that accumulated leadership wisdom and influence *before* you retire will help soften whatever butt kicks may come when the gates of your career close.

Butt-Kicking Tips for Senior Leaders

The good news is, if you're a senior leader, odds are you've had your butt kicked many times over the years, perhaps even by a few pipsqueak whippersnappers—so you won't get too upset when I kick you with these tips.

> **Get over yourself.** Yes, yes, we all know you boot-strapped your career from the ground up, you earned everything you've gotten, and without you this company would be nothing. But guess what? We don't care. And neither should you. We love you best when you're just being you, minus the martyrdom.

> **Experience the world of the young 'uns.** Yup, the greenhorns don't do things the way you and your generation did. They cut corners, slough off, and kiss too much butt. But remember, you did all of that, too, early in your career. Plus, new leaders today are way more tech savvy, are tapped into a global community, are helping the company be socially conscious, and are doing a better job of having an outside-of-work identity than you ever did. Do yourself a favor: get closer to their world instead of expecting them to reside in yours.

> **Mentor more.** You've still got a lot of value to add, especially when it comes to mentoring new leaders. There's a good chance that your own career was advanced by many leader intercessors along the way. Now it's your turn to be a pivot person. New leaders need seasoned leaders to become good leaders. Plus, your legacy depends on it!

> **Divert your power.** The gates are closing on your career, but that doesn't mean you won't be able to apply your leadership influence. If you're not

serving on a nonprofit board already, do so. Your
community needs your wisdom, connections, and
influence! Find places to serve at VolunteerMatch
.org, Idealist.org, and Bridgespan.org. See, you big
beluga, you still matter!

PART III

Leading, for Worse or for Better

S ome leaders get, and deserve, more ass kicks than others. This section will introduce you to two sadly common leadership archetypes: *Pigheads* and *Weaklings*. Leaders who are overly sure of, and preoccupied with, themselves eventually reap the butt-kicking consequences of arrogance. Conversely, leaders who are impish, fickle, and banal get booted due to ineffectiveness. The two leading causes of leadership butt kicks are over- and under-confidence.

When confidence and humility are present in the right measure, your leadership strength, influence, and enjoyment will grow. As it does, you'll become more adept at blending confidence and humility in ways that better serve the people you're leading. This section will introduce you to three important leadership roles: the *Loyal Rebel*, the *Velvet Hammer*, and the *Genuine Faker*.

This section also covers

➤ the negative impacts of leadership arrogance and weakness,

➤ how weakness is often withheld or unused strength,

➤ how self-respect is balanced between self-absorption and self-neglect,

➤ why having a "right-sized" ego is more important than having a big or small one,

➤ why being a Loyal Rebel, Velvet Hammer, and Genuine Faker is important to leading with confidence and humility.

The results you get as a leader, as well as the ass kicks you cause, will be directly related to the presence or absence of confidence and humility.

CHAPTER **6**

Kick-Worthy Leaders
Pigheads and Weaklings

The whole problem with the world is that fools
and fanatics are always so certain of themselves,
and wiser people so full of doubts.

—Bertrand Russell

All leaders will experience a kick in the ass at some point in their careers. No leader gets to escape that uncomfortable reality. That said, there are two distinct types of leaders whose butt kicks are particularly forceful and largely self-inflicted. If you've been in the workforce for a while, you've likely worked with one or both of these dysfunctional leaders at some point in your career. It's a soul-sucking experience you won't soon forget. The wreckage they cause is real and lasting, and generally unstoppable except by a painful butt kick. Fortunately, for these two leader archetypes especially, butt kicks are inevitable. Get ready to meet the leaders you probably already know and wish you didn't: Pigheads and Weaklings.

Oh Lord, It's Hard to Be Humble . . .

Some years ago, I was facilitating the kickoff of a multi-year leadership program. Thirty emerging leaders had been selected for the program by the company's senior leaders. The program, which is on its fifth iteration, is well established as a leader spawning ground within the company. If you're lucky enough to be selected as a participant, there's a good chance that you'll be in a senior leadership role someday.

As a kickoff event, I invited each of the new participants to share a little about him- or herself, including what he or she hoped to get out of the experience. Most talked about wanting to strengthen their leadership impact so they could add more value to the company, or leave a legacy by inspiring other people to seek leadership roles. All went as expected until it was Gerald's turn to introduce himself. "My aim is to share what I know about leadership with my fellow classmates. You've probably heard that I graduated from West Point and spent time in Iraq. I've literally learned about leadership from some of the greatest leaders alive, and I plan on sharing what I've learned as we go through the program together. I believe that with great leadership comes great responsibility. When you've learned something important you need to pass it on to others. My hope is that some of what I learned will help you be better leaders."

As Gerald spoke, I spied the reaction of his classmates. It was as if he had just bellowed a large burp while singing "God Bless America." It struck exactly the wrong note, at exactly the wrong time, in exactly the wrong way. A few people visibly winced, as if they had just whiffed stale cheese. Gerald, through his flatulent introduction, showed that he was exactly the wrong choice for the program. The program was about leadership. Gerald was about himself. Gerald is a Pighead.

Now, don't get me wrong. I've included many, many ex-military leaders in programs that I've designed and led. The program that Gerald was part of, for example, incorporated a talk by Captain John McBride, a navy pilot and former NASA space shuttle astronaut. That same program also included Dr. Henry L. "Dick" Thompson, a Vietnam vet who is a renowned expert on stress management. Recent programs have included Captain John Havlik, who retired after twenty-nine years as a Navy SEAL, and Steve Romano, a retired FBI hostage negotiator and a decorated air force officer. Additionally, a number of program participants themselves are ex-military, including one participant whose body has *seven* bullet holes from the time he spent in the first war in Iraq (his nickname was the Human Shield!). I admire all of these people, and many more ex-military folks with whom I've worked and whom I've known.

What made Gerald's introduction so pigheaded had zero to do with his being a military vet. Rather, it was how completely condescending he was. He put himself above his classmates, basically saying, *I know a lot more about leadership than you do, and you are fortunate that I plan on blessing you with what I've learned.*

How do you think Gerald did in the program? How well do you expect he bonded with his classmates? Within two months he quit the program and the company. Pass the cheese!

The Pigheaded Leader

There is no bigger turnoff than arrogance. This is especially true of leadership. Followers will afford a leader a lot of power as long as they know that power is tethered to humility. People want to know that no matter how

much success you've achieved, no matter how much influence and authority you have, you haven't forgotten
your roots. They want to know that you wear right-sized
britches and that you put them on the same way they do.
But if a leader's ego becomes inflated and untethered from
the grounding influence of humility, followers will unfol-
low the leader fast.

For a host of reasons, it's easy to get seduced into
thinking you're special when you're in a position of leadership. First, leaders are in smaller numbers, so it makes
them comparatively rare. Not everyone gets to be one. Second, leaders get more perks. They get bigger titles, bigger
workspaces, and bigger salaries. Naturally, bigger egos
can follow. Finally, leaders get a lot more behavioral latitude. Nobody challenges them when they show up late for
a meeting, interrupt people, or skirt company policies
with which employees at lower levels have to comply. For
example, the senior executives of one company I worked
with instituted a company-wide time-reporting system so
that the minute-by-minute actions of employees could be
accounted for, but exempted themselves from having to
use the system, explaining that their time fluctuated too
much to accurately monitor. Poor babies!

Given the special treatment leaders get, is it any wonder that some begin to think of themselves as the focal
point of leadership rather than the people they're leading?
They think they're special because, well, they are—at least
according to the construct of leadership as it exists in
most workplaces. It takes an enormous amount of leadership self-discipline and restraint to keep your ego in check
when the idea that you're special is constantly being rein-

forced. It's well worth doing, though. Arrogant leadership rarely engenders true loyalty. Followers quickly lose faith in a leader who cares more about enlarging his power than their well-being. Leadership arrogance nearly always leads to follower disloyalty.

It takes an enormous amount of leadership self-discipline and restraint to keep your ego in check when the idea that you're special is constantly being reinforced.

Oblivious Swine

In my experience working with thousands of leaders, I have found that nearly all are ethical and honest people. They genuinely want to do right by their organizations and people. Decency is the norm. While exceedingly rare, the ethics of some leaders become twisted when they become drunk on their own specialness. The human ego is capable of breathtaking levels of obliviousness when overly inflated. For example, I was once part of a leadership conference lineup that included the CEO of a famous mattress company. Before the event, one of my copresenters gave me a heads up: "Watch out, his ego walks in the room thirty minutes before he does." Sure enough, when it was the CEO's time to speak, he bragged about how he was able to dominate his board, about the risks he was taking that his predecessor didn't, and how he had hired some of his own family members because he knew they had the right DNA. To top it off, at the end of his talk he gave everyone a copy of his favorite book of quotations. The only person quoted in the book was himself.

To be a Pighead means to be narcissistic, cocksure, and self-oblivious. It also means to justify your own ignorant behavior with *rational lies* (rationalize). What the CEO never mentioned to the conference attendees, but that the *New York Times* eventually uncovered, was that the CEO spent hardly any time at the company's headquarters, preferring instead to rule from his opulent home in Naples, Florida, or aboard his eighty-foot yacht—the one with eleven televisions.

Sadly, the pig heads of some leaders are so thick that even a giant kick in the ass doesn't dent their egos enough to cause them to change. I'm sure, for example, the mattress company CEO could concoct a contorted defense of the $40 million compensation he received when the company was sold as part of a bankruptcy proceeding. *Well, the company never would have gone bankrupt if more people had led like me!*

The Weakling Leader

Leadership is often a function of dominance; if your talent or personality outdominates that of your peers, you're more likely to be tapped for leadership roles than they are. Because of this, a Weakling leader may, for a time, be less identifiable than his or her Pigheaded counterparts. The Weakling leader did *something*, after all, to deserve a leadership position. Whereas Pigheads are bold and obvious, though, the ineffective nature of Weakling leaders takes longer to be revealed. Think, for example, of the most arrogant leader you ever worked for. Now think of the weakest leader you ever worked for. The Pighead comes to mind much quicker than the Weakling, right?

One hallmark of Weakling leadership is an unwilling-
ness to take risks, or, put another way, a tendency to place
too much emphasis on playing it safe. This behavior
shows up in a number of ways. During meetings, for example, a Weakling leader will rarely state his or her actual
preference or opinion. Instead, he will wait until more-
senior leaders have spoken, sizing up the wind direction,
and then recite what his bosses said after changing the
words around a little to give them a veneer of originality.
Instead of reasonably evaluating their views, he adopts
them, wholesale. In the process, he avoids having to develop or defend his own considered opinion. If you don't
offer up your own ideas, views, and opinions, no one can
subject them to scrutiny. It's a camouflage trick that cre-
ates the illusion of presence; you get to appear at the table
while the true you remains safely invisible.

Once the Weakling leader has appropriated the views
and opinions of his or her bosses, deferring to the bosses'
preferences becomes an easy excuse when decisions are
questioned by the Weakling's direct reports. Even if the
Weakling herself has misgivings about the decisions, when
quizzed about it by her own direct reports, she is apt to
say, "Because that's what our senior leadership said they
want, so we just have to do it." Once again the camouflage
trick is played. *Look, I am here acting as a thoughtful and
independent leader, but really I'm a hollow sycophant!*

Weakness Is Retention of Strength
Weakness, in the case of the Weakling leader, does not always equate with not being strong. In fact, a lot of Weakling leaders are actually quite strong. But they withhold
their strength. Like a human dam, they hold back their

true preferences, desires, and dissenting opinions. No, it's not lack of strength that burdens some Weakling leaders; it's *fear* in all its malevolent forms: fear of displeasing authority, fear of being cast out of the group, fear of messing up, fear of being "found out" as an imposter, and fear of success and being obliged to meet perpetually escalating performance standards, to name a few. The more immersed in fear the Weakling leader is, the more withheld he is likely to be. Fear inhibits the willing expression of strength.

By withholding the full potency of her potential, the Weakling leader gyps herself and the company. For example, I recently participated in a performance feedback meeting between a CEO of a building company and one of his direct reports, the director of the company's safety department. The safety director had been bucking for a VP title because he felt it would give him more clout with the division leaders, field personnel, and customers. The CEO said no, explaining that while the safety director did a solid job of ensuring compliance with company and industry safety standards, when it came to being a leader, he played it too safe. His withholding was especially noticeable during the monthly meeting of the company's executive safety counsel, which was attended by the company's most senior executives (VPs, EVPs, and the CEO). Though the safety director was the meeting leader, he rarely spoke up, and struggled to corral the executives and keep the meetings on track. "Listen," the CEO continued, "I need you to stop being a good soldier, and I need you to start being a general. You show strength when it comes to dealing with your peers and direct reports, but when it comes to pushing back on me and my team, you hold back.

KICKASS COMEBACKS: Perp Edition

Michael Milken made his money the old-fashioned way—he cheated! Not that he needed to: he was a Phi Beta Kappa graduate of the University of California at Berkeley, and held an MBA from the Wharton School at the University of Pennsylvania. By the late 1980s, Milken had the highest-ranking income in the United States, earning over $250 million a year as a bond dealer for Drexel Burnham Lambert. He was hugely instrumental in the popularization of high-yield bonds—more infamously known as "junk bonds." During the late 1980s, Milken was known as the "junk bond king."

Milken's whip-smart knowledge of the bond industry enabled him to stay ahead of pesky investigators from the Securities and Exchange Commission. It wasn't until he was personally identified by infamous stock trader Ivan Boesky that Milken was caught. Boesky had fingered Milken as part of a plea deal for a security fraud and insider trading investigation that had snagged Boesky. Milken plead guilty to racketeering and reporting violations, and received a $600 million fine and a ten-year prison sentence.

The day after getting out of jail, the now-disgraced Milken was diagnosed with prostate cancer. The "C" word, however, would provide Milken with a new point of focus for his sharp mind. Though barred from the security industry for life, he was still rich, smart, and well connected. He founded the Prostate Cancer Foundation, which fast became the largest source of philanthropic funds for prostate cancer research. In the process, he developed a new model of stimulating research by investing directly in therapy-driven ideas instead of basic science, holding researchers accountable for results, and monitoring impact metrics. Before long, other research charities were influenced by the "Milken model," including the Juvenile Diabetes Research Foundation, the

Cystic Fibrosis Foundation, and the Michael J. Fox Foundation, which aims for a cure for Parkinson's disease.

Since being released from jail, the bulk of Milken's time, energy, and money has been devoted to philanthropy.

Sources: Jeffery Sonnenfeld and Andrew Ward, "Firing Back: How Great Leaders Rebound after Career Disasters," *Harvard Business Review,* January 2007, https://hbr.org/2007/01/firing-back-how-great-leaders-rebound-after-career-disasters; Kurt Eichenwald, "Milken Set to Pay $600 Million Fine in Wall St. Fraud," *New York Times,* April 21, 1990, http://www.nytimes.com/1990/04/21/business/milken-set-to-pay-a-600-million-fine-in-wall-st-fraud.html?pagewanted=all.

Right now you're only a half leader—you lead down but not up. You need to assert yourself more and take more risks with my group. You need to put your ass out there so the execs see that you have a stake in the game. You'll never become the safety VP unless you play it less safe."

I Know I Should, But . . .

One difference between Weaklings and Pigheads is that Weakling leaders are not oblivious. They are often fully conscious about what the right course of action is; they just don't take it. Right actions are often hard actions, and Weaklings avoid what is hard. They know what they *should* do; they just don't do it. Interpersonal confrontation is a good example. Leaders have to set standards and assert boundaries, and that occasionally requires confronting people who don't meet standards or who violate boundaries. Weaklings avoid the interpersonal funkiness that accompanies confronting others, which causes them to be viewed as even weaker.

For example, I once worked with a conflict-avoiding C-level executive who was boss to a confrontational, yet highly talented, senior manager. The senior manager's job required gathering data from multiple departments to create trend reports for the C-suite executives. Almost as an extension of the importance of the reports themselves, the senior manager carried herself like the chief constable in a city of delinquents. But instead of carrying a billy club, she threw her power around in a way that intimidated and grated on people. Even the other C-level execs, who were the leaders of the department leaders, were rankled by the senior manager's obnoxious ways. Her behavior had gone on for years. Yet, despite knowing full well about all the feathers the manager ruffled, and despite having implored her to be more diplomatic multiple times, her C-level boss couldn't muster up the courage to fire her. He rationalized that the value she added outweighed the damage she caused.

Pigheads grow more pigheaded around Weaklings, and Weaklings get weaker around Pigheads. The longer the C-level exec postponed firing the senior manager, the harder it became to do, because even as she grew in her obnoxiousness, she also grew in her skills, competency, and expertise. Firing her became increasingly more consequential and risky. Yet by not firing her, the C-level felt guilty for not doing what he knew he should.

The Big Difference

The main difference between Pigheads and Weaklings is that Pigheads are self-absorbed and Weaklings are self-neglectful. Both are in need of an ego adjustment.

Until a Pighead reaps the consequences that too much pride inevitably brings, he will remain oblivious to the

Pigheads versus Weaklings

	Pigheads	Weaklings
Leadership view	➡ My way is right, your way is wrong ➡ Look at what I did	➡ I'll do what you want ➡ Don't ask me
Disposition	➡ Stand out	➡ Hide out
View of others	➡ Others are weak	➡ Others are less weak than me
Fears	➡ Losing ➡ Not getting his way ➡ Loss of control ➡ Being disrespected ➡ Caring for others and being obliged to focus on them	➡ Displeasing bosses ➡ Exposing true opinions ➡ Not belonging ➡ Being found out as an imposter ➡ Success and being obliged to meet escalating standards
Damage to self	➡ Loss of potential learning gained from self-awareness and introspection	➡ Loss of self-respect for not sticking up for oneself
Damage to organization	➡ Wreckage in the form of high turnover, low morale, unused potential of others	➡ Untapped strength that could be applied for the good of the organization or people within it
Butt kicks needed	➡ Kicks that shatter the oversized ego ➡ Kicks that instigate humility	➡ Kicks that expose the withheld potential ➡ Kicks that inspire assertiveness

negative impact that his oversized ego causes. He'll be oblivious to the diminished loyalty, thwarted ideas, and resentful feelings that he has caused among those being led. Yet, despite the enormous damage a Pighead can do, we should have pity on him. The thickness of his skull, and the denseness of his ego, makes personal enlightenment next to impossible. Unless his ego gets a jarring butt kick, he'll be relegated to a life of obliviousness.

Until a Weakling exposes her point of view to the light of day, until she asserts herself even among more dominant or senior leaders, and until she stands up for what is right instead of what is popular, the Weakling will always withhold strength. What makes a Weakling also pitiable is the withheld potential and unapplied potency that could serve the good of the company and the people being led by the Weakling. Minus a forceful butt kick, the Weakling leader becomes increasingly impotent.

Take Your Medicine

Every leader carries a dormant germ of a Pighead and a Weakling inside. They represent the two opposing strains of leadership influenza that every leader needs to guard against for fear of activating them. Once you succumb to either type of behavior, recovering your leadership health is nearly impossible without a swift kick in the tail. Butt kicks are harsh antidotes for Pigheads and Weaklings, and they don't always work.

In the next chapter you'll learn about how too much or too little confidence leads to pigheaded and weak behavior, as well as the butt kicks that are prone to follow. You'll also learn about the importance of having a "right-sized" ego, getting the right proportion of confidence and humility for you. In the meantime, here are some tips to keep your leadership healthy and free from the ill effects of pride and impotence.

Pighead Prevention Tips

➤ **Get out of yourself.** List all the people who have influenced your leadership beliefs and describe the impact they had on you. Reach out to at least three of those people to thank them for the mark they left on you.

➤ **Lead on behalf of others.** Identify the leadership impact you hope to have on others when you apply your leadership influence. Identify three specific actions you can take to positively impact others within the next two weeks.

➤ **Invite feedback slaps.** Get unfiltered feedback about yourself by enlisting an executive coach, taking a personality survey, going through a 360-degree feedback process, or entering therapy.

➤ **Shut your piehole.** Let others have the limelight. Invite others to comment when decisions are being made. Seek the input or review of others before issuing major directives. Ask more questions than you answer. Constantly be asking yourself, "Why am I talking?" (**WAIT**).

Weakling Prevention Tips

➤ **Tally the cost of withheld strength.** Identify the strengths that you might be withholding from applying. Tally the cost of your withheld strength. What has holding back cost your career? What might it be costing those you're leading?

➤ **Have *personal fidelity*.** Identify the stronger leader you'd be proud to be. How is that leader different from the leader you are today? Identify three actions you can take to close the gap. Be faithful to your future leader self.

➤ **Get courageously unsafe.** Ask yourself, "In what ways am I playing it too safe at work?" Based on your answer, identify three specific actions that would nudge you outside your comfort zone. Moving into discomfort causes you to confront fear and will build your courage and your confidence.

➤ **Speak up already!** Sit down with a notepad and a pen and write down your point of view about leadership. Do the same about current decisions that are under way in your organization. State your points of view at the next appropriate occasion. Let your bosses know your thoughts, especially if they run counter to the group. Speak more truth.

CHAPTER 7

A More Perfect Derrière

Confident Humility

You learn more from getting your butt
kicked than getting it kissed.

—Tom Hanks

Most butt kicks are the natural consequence of a leader's accumulated behavior over time. Often, they are an inevitable response to exaggerated hubris or withering meekness. You're most likely to get them when you're overly prideful or anemically weak. Butt kicks are life's mysterious and painful way of reminding us of the dangers of too much or too little confidence.

Overconfidence

When we believe in ourselves more than we should, when we put more stock in our skills and capabilities than they actually warrant, when we start all tasks from the presumption that "I got this," overconfidence begins to distort our leadership. Overconfidence causes us to make decisions impulsively fast. Overconfidence causes us to trust our judgment over the judgment of others. And overconfidence causes us to be dismissive toward those whom we perceive as slowing us down or not having the power to further our goals. The most obvious and embellished example of overconfidence is the Pighead leader, who often steps over (or on!) people she views as getting in the way of her goals. Her motto is, "If you're not part of the bulldozer, you're part of the pavement." Butt kicks stemming from overconfidence are the natural blowback of selfish leadership, often coming in the form of backstabbing or betrayal by the people we have led (or, more often, *mis*led). As Julius Caesar said, "Et tu, Brute?"

Underconfidence

When we are preoccupied with the potential for failure at the start of every task, when we hyperfocus on risk mitigation, and when we continually delay decisions by deferring them for others' approval, underconfidence is at work. Underconfidence causes us to be timid, hesitant, and unoriginal. When we lack confidence, we don't trust our ideas, much less fight for them. We cede to the ideas, perspectives, and preferences of others. Consequently, we lose the opportunity to shape decisions and effect change. It is underconfidence, as you might have guessed, that causes the Weakling leader to lack backbone. The Weakling leader defends neither himself nor those he is leading (or *mis*leading!). Butt kicks stemming from prolonged underconfidence are often connected to loss of respect among your bosses, your peers, those you're leading, and ultimately, yourself. When you don't take steps to build your own confidence, you are disrespecting yourself. Collectively, the hesitancy, timidity, indecision, and lack of respect caused by underconfidence add up to loss of both leadership potency and relevance.

Confident Humility

A leader's choice of how to lead needs to take into account what followers will follow. Followers won't follow leaders who lead through intimidation and who don't care about them. They also won't follow weakness and cowardice. Most especially, they won't follow leaders who diminish them and make them feel small. What they *will* follow is a leader who embodies strong values, paints a clear and hopeful vision of the future, acts with reasonability and composure, solicits and acts on their input, and makes people feel proud of themselves. Followers follow leaders who are *confidently humble*.

For our leadership to be assertive, decisive, and firm, we need to have confidence. For our leadership to be authentic, giving, and supportive, we need to have humility. Confidence and humility are complementary and counterbalancing forces that fortify the potency of leadership. When our actions are directed by confidence and humility, we are truly operating out of our best self. The leadership ideal, then, is to become a leader who is both highly confident and genuinely humble. You've gotten to this place when you respect those you lead as much as you respect yourself.

What does a confidently humble leader look like? First, she is comfortable in her own skin. That comfort stems from the self-respect that seasoning and experience provide. She knows that she has earned her place. She has capitalized on the lessons she learned from all of the butt kickings she's had along the way. Her self-worth doesn't come from what others think about her; it comes from living in alignment with a value system that she honors and upholds. Principles matter to her, providing a source of strength and guiding her decisions and choices. The confidently humble leader states her views assertively and constructively, not to trump others, but to add her perspective. When situations require, she can be forceful and direct, but never in a way that is demeaning toward others. To her, people are not objects. The people she is leading make her job meaningful and worthwhile, and their growth and development are how she assesses her effectiveness.

The confidently humble leader knows that she doesn't have all the answers, and doesn't expect herself to. She is eager to get the input, perspective, and help of the people she's leading, and knows that they are eager to give it. Her leadership isn't threatened by strong opinions or personalities. Above all, she values people who are candid, thoughtful, and authentic. She, too, is all those things.

| | Confident Humility | |
| Self-Absorption | (Self-Respect) | Self-Neglect |

Ego

Being Right-Sized

The beauty and gift of a butt kick is that it right-sizes our ego. When we're overconfident, our butt kicks humble us. When we're underconfident, our butt kicks inspire us to take actions that build our confidence. Butt kicks act as a correcting device, ensuring that our confidence and humility are proportional.

That is not to say that each leader should equally carry the same amount of confidence or humility. The proportion

KICKASS COMEBACKS: Crackerjack Edition

When Yankees owner George Steinbrenner hired Joe Torre as the team's manager, the *New York Daily News* ran with the headline, "Clueless Joe." Until that point, the 894 wins Torre had under his belt were eclipsed by his 1,003 losses. Torre had just been fired from the Saint Louis Cardinals due to his lackluster performance. Understandably, Yankees fans viewed his hiring as a colossal mistake.

Torre, fortunately, had been seasoned by all his loses. As he put it, "Unless you have bad times, you can't appreciate the good times." A New Yorker himself, Torre quickly gained the respect of the team. He knew that managing the Yankees also meant managing Steinbrenner, the brutal New York media, and the scrutinizing fans.

Torre gained a reputation as a leader with an admirable blend of confidence and humility. Unlike more feisty or pugnacious Yankees managers like Billy Martin, Torre led with a steady hand and intense focus. He would go on to lead the Yankees to twelve straight playoff appearances, winning the World Series four times. The Hall of Famer is widely considered to be the most beloved manager to ever wear the Yankees pinstripes.

In 2002, Torre and his wife, Ali, established the Joe Torre Safe at Home Foundation. The foundation provides resources and education about domestic violence. Torre's father was a New York City police detective who, unbeknownst to the city residents who revered him, physically and emotionally abused Joe and his siblings. The foundation now runs "safe rooms" in a growing number of schools, where children who are growing up in similar households can meet with a professional counselor who is trained in domestic violence intervention.

Taking stock of how his winning and losing on and off the field had seasoned him, Torre said, "I think that I have a sensitivity toward people, and that is a strength."

Sources: "Clueless Joe," *New York Daily News*, November 3, 1995, http://www.nydailynews.com/sports/baseball/yankees/ex-yankees-manager-joe-torre-front-back-pages-clueless-joe-bombers-legend-gallery-1.55145?pmSlide=1.56363; Joe Giglio, "Baseball Hall of Fame 2014: A Look Back on the Biggest Joe Torre Stories," NJ.com, July 27, 2014, http://www.nj.com/yankees/index.ssf/2014/07/baseball_hall_of_fame_2014_a_look_back_on_the_biggest_joe_torre_stories.html; Joe Torre Safe at Home Foundation website, http://www.JoeTorre.org; "Joe Torre," National Baseball Hall of Fame, http://baseballhall.org/hof/torre-joe.

should be unique to each leader. It should also factor in the situation the leader faces. If you have a six-foot ego but five-foot capabilities, you will drown walking across a six-foot-deep lake. Likewise, if you have a five-foot ego but six-foot capabilities, you'll bang your head on a lot of doorframes. We are less dangerous to ourselves and others when our levels of confidence and humility are right-sized according to our capabilities, talents, experience, and shortcomings.

A Right-Sized You

Think for a moment about the leader you most admire. Pick someone you've actually worked with, not someone on the world stage. Didn't that leader possess both *confidence* and *humility* in good measure? Didn't that leader treat you the way he or she treated him- or herself? Now how about you and your leadership? Are you comfortable in your own skin? Are you slow to judge others and quick to solicit their input? Is bringing people along with you and engaging them around goals more important than having your authority respected? Would you say you have high levels of both confidence and humility? Would the people you lead say so too? What follows are some tips for building confidence and becoming humble.

Tips for Building Right-Sized Confidence

➤ **Increase competency.** Confidence grows when your skills are sharp. You're more likely to be confident when you're highly competent. Leaders don't have to be good at everything. But you have to be good at *something*. What would others say you're really good at? Take what you're already good at and bring those skills to an even higher level of mastery.

➤ **Walk through your fears.** Fear inhibits confidence. Conversely, taking action despite being afraid—the simplest definition of the word *courage*—builds our confidence. List your top three work fears, then identify three specific courageous actions that you could take to confront each one. Confidence grows when you act with courage.

➤ **Get physically fit.** Too many workaholic careerists are physically lazy. Take care of yourself by exercising, eating healthy, not smoking, not drinking to excess, and getting enough sleep. Being good to yourself is the first step toward being good to others. Self-respect builds confidence.

➤ **Build confidence in others.** Give what you get. The point of being more confident isn't to acquire more personal power; it's to be a source of power for others. Identify someone who could use more confidence, perhaps a struggling emerging leader. Tell them that you're interested in their success and, with their permission, you'd like to partner with them to help them succeed.

Tips for Having Right-Sized Humility

➤ **Stand next to something big.** There's something humbling about standing by the ocean, or gazing out over a massive canyon, or looking up at the starry infinity on a cold night. Doing these things helps you remember that you're not the center of the universe; you are just a speck. Never forget that!

➤ **Get spiritually fit.** The great spiritual traditions are founded on virtues that emphasize modesty, personal goodness, and selflessness. Being spiritually fit is the best way to have a transcendent experience, which helps us rise above our petty selfishness and become a more generous member of the human community.

➤ **Serve others.** It's hard to be self-absorbed when you're focused on serving others. Get out of yourself by spending time with those whose needs are greater than yours. The options are endless: volunteer at a homeless shelter, serve as a Big Brother or Big Sister, help out at a Special Olympics event. But you have to actually do it. Sending a check is a poor and lazy substitute.

When your confidence and humility are right-sized for you, you'll start developing a more grounded and authentic leadership style. The more genuine confidence and humility you have, the less likely butt kicks become. In the next chapter, you'll learn about three major leadership roles that, to differing degrees, are fortified by confidence and humility.

CHAPTER 8

Three Expressions of Confident Humility

If I only had a little humility, I would be perfect.
—Ted Turner

Butt-Kick Prevention

The more genuinely confident and humble you are, the less likely you'll be to get kicked in the ass. That's because, as mentioned, most butt kicks are self-inflicted behavioral boomerangs, the result of behaving with too much arrogance or too little strength. This chapter introduces three leadership roles that draw on, and are strengthened by, confidence and humility. They reflect the essential behaviors that differentiate a leader from everyone else. Consider them a form of butt-kick prevention, because when you mix confidence and humility in the right measure, they ward off arrogance and weakness . . . and butt kicks.

The Loyal Rebel

Hines Brannan was the best leader I ever worked for. Hines was a partner at Accenture and, at the time, was overseeing the largest outsourcing engagement in the history of the world. BellSouth had hired Accenture to manage over seven hundred IT applications. Hines led thirty-five partners, who in turn provided leadership to an organization of over two thousand Accenture employees, most of whom BellSouth had outsourced to Accenture. I was a middle manager in Accenture's change management and human performance practice, and I reported directly to Hines. I was part chief of staff and part gofer. But I loved the job because it allowed me to work closely with Hines and interact with all of his leaders. Until then, I had never worked for a leader who lived up to the leader ideals that I had studied in graduate school. What made Hines so unique, and so unlike some of the other partners that I had experienced, was that he was a wonderful blend of company loyalist and independent rebel.

Earlier in his career, before Andersen Consulting renamed itself Accenture, Hines took over as the managing partner of the company's regional office in Charlotte, North Carolina. His predecessor, George Shaheen—who would later become the company's CEO—had required his partners to attend a weekly status meeting that ran from seven till noon on Saturday mornings. Because consulting partners travel intensely, Shaheen reasoned that Saturday was the only day he could get them all together. The consequence, though, was that many partners would only be home on Saturday afternoon and evening before heading back out on the road on Sunday.

In his first official act as the Charlotte office's managing partner, Hines gathered all the partners and promptly told them there would no longer be any Saturday morning meetings. He wanted them to be with their families

and enjoy their free time. The partners gave Hines a standing ovation as the meeting was quickly dismissed.

Too many leaders become little more than agents of
a larger system, reflexively carrying out commands from
above. They go along to get along, subsuming their originality, objectivity, and independence in service to the
organization. In the worst examples, they become fully
compromised leader lemmings, yessing those above, and
expecting yes from those below. When enough lemmings
hold sway, politics starts to trump principles, and what is
convenient and expedient gets chosen over what is right
but risky. The perpetuation of *what is* gets valued above
the pursuit of *what can be*, and the preservation of the
status quo—including the current leaders' place within
it—prevails. This is how "the establishment" is born, complete with its "We've always done it this way" mentality. A
new leader who doesn't quickly get in line is marginalized
until she does, and if she doesn't, the establishment apparatus shake their heads, mumbling, "She wasn't a good fit,"
as they show her the door. What they really mean is she
was too independent, too noncompliant, too uppity—she
was a threat to order, control, and ultimately the establishment itself.

What made me admire Hines so much was his blend of
confidence and humility. He was humble enough to know
he existed within a larger system of authority, of which he
was a member, and confident enough to act independently
of that system when warranted. He had seen the personal
toll that overwork had taken on the lives and marriages
of the partners. The Saturday meetings, in Hines's mind,
were symptomatic of a perverse work obsessiveness, and,

ultimately, hurt peoples' productivity and well-being. A lot of managing partners in other regional offices also required Saturday morning partner meetings, and, despite the pressure to conform, Hines wouldn't be one of them. To him it was a matter of principle. His job was to protect his partners so they could be healthy and productive, regardless of distorted cultural norms that wrongly equated the quantity of time spent at work with quality of output. Hines cared too much about the company and its partners to allow workaholic lunacy to push sanity out the office door. Hines was a Loyal Rebel—a member of the executive body who was capable of acting independently of it when its own interests were served by doing so.

You, as a Rebel Loyalist

In most organizations, the moment you become responsible for leading others, you cross over into the management ranks. The shift represents a sort of threshold where, once you cross over, you become a member of the executive body. This crossover is often represented by the word "made"—as in, you "made" manager, meaning you made it from the nonmanagement to the management ranks. As a member of the executive body, you're expected to be even more loyal to the company's values, strategic agenda, and written and unwritten rules.

Loyalty is a good thing. By giving it, you gain trust. But the loyalty you give to the company often requires suspending some of your own wants and preferences. Even your own values may have to be compromised, at least to some degree. Loyalty is something you *give*, and in exchange for giving your loyalty to the organization, and by extension sublimating your loyalty to self, you get to be more involved in shaping decisions. All of this is to say, loyalty is connected to humility because it requires surrendering some of yourself to the agenda of the executive body. This only makes sense, because if every leader were to put his or her wants and preferences above the organization's, nothing would ever get done.

Balanced against the need to be loyal is the need to be independent-minded. As a leader, you're expected to assert bold ideas, imaginatively solve problems, and be decisive. At least in healthy organizations, you're also expected to push back against directives that are unethical, or off-mission, or disconnected from the organization's values. Being a rebel leader means acting in the organization's best interest when others aren't doing so. You have to be enough of a maverick to sometimes break rules, especially when the sanity of an exception outweighs the insanity of allegiance to them. Doing the right thing often requires being disloyal to the wrong rule for the right reasons. When Hines canceled the Saturday morning meetings, he was breaking with a common practice within the company because it was unhealthy for the partners and the company.

Being a Loyal Rebel means having enough confidence to act with independence, and enough humility to put the interests of the organization above your own. Here are some tips to help you become a Loyal Rebel:

> ➤ **Be loyal to the rebel founder.** If you go back far enough in your organization's history, you'll likely find someone who bucked convention, went against

the tide, and did something disruptive in the marketplace. Know that rebel's story. What rules did he or she break? What did he or she have to sacrifice in order to create the organization? How did loyalty factor into his or her success? Who or what was he or she most loyal to? What did he or she have to become disloyal to? In what ways does the spirit of that person live on in the organization's written or unwritten values? What attributes of the founder are worth adopting? What attributes do you have already?

➤ **Check your beliefs.** Which beliefs have you adopted without scrutiny? Many people, for example, follow the same religion of their parents for no other reason than habit. It's okay to follow the religious beliefs and practices of your parents, just as long as *you* actually believe them. The same is true for leadership. What do you actually believe about leadership? How were those beliefs shaped, and who or what shaped them? Having independence of thought requires codifying your own beliefs. Answer this key question: What do you truly believe about what it takes to lead people?

➤ **Determine whom you are with, and who is with you.** Just as critical as the ancient question *Who am I?* is the question *Whom am I* with? Who at work stands with you when situations go south? Whom can you be yourself around, without fear of being judged? Who always has your back? Who's the bloke who will tell you when you've got parsley

stuck in your teeth at lunch? Who can call BS on
you when you're deceiving yourself? Stick with
those people. Find more like them. Build a posse
worthy of your loyalty.

➤ **Get clear on the rules and the exceptions.** Check to
see if your organization has a code of ethics. If so,
scrutinize them inside out. Understand why each
individual code was included. Learn what extenuat-
ing circumstances or exceptions would fall outside
the code. If your organization doesn't have a formal
code of ethics, assert yourself by floating the idea of
establishing one. Be a rebel and lead the charge to
create the rules!

The Velvet Hammer

Sister Rosemary Connelly is the executive director of
Misericordia, a Catholic charity where over one thousand
staff members serve some six hundred children and adults
who have developmental disabilities or physical challenges. The mission of Misericordia, which sits on a thirty-
one-acre campus in Chicago, is to maximize the level of
independence and self-determination of its special-needs
clients by providing an environment that fosters spiritual-
ity, dignity, respect, and enhancement of quality of life.
Misericordia's clients come from diverse racial, religious,
and socioeconomic backgrounds, and part of the charity's
mission is to help them become good citizens. The restau-
rant, gift shop, and bakery are all staffed by its special-
needs clients. Sister Rosemary is a force of nature, at once
Misericordia's beloved leader, chief fund-raiser, and political arm-twister.

The stories about Sister Rosemary's feisty ways are legion. Here's one that captures how well she mixes assertiveness with diplomacy. A few years ago, Chicago's blunt-talking mayor Rahm Emanuel decided to start charging a fee to Chicago nonprofits that used the city water system. As a consequence, Misericordia's water bill instantly went from zero to $300,000. Not long after, Sister Rosemary invited the mayor to be the featured keynote speaker at a fund-raising breakfast at Misericorida. As the event was getting started, she took the microphone and noted that unlike in years past, everyone would have to go without water during breakfast due to cutbacks the charity had to make to pay the new water fee the mayor had levied. Then, with a twinkle in her eyes, she introduced the red-faced mayor. The mayor, whose intimidating ways earned him the nickname "Rahm the Impaler," stammered before dishing out some ribbing of his own, "I thought Jewish mothers had the corner on the market as it relates to guilt."

The two actually enjoy a very warm relationship. Mayor Emanuel even donned a chef's hat and served french toast at a Misericordia fund-raiser a few years later. His challah bread french toast was the winning recipe. Still, as genuinely good-spirited as the relationship between the mayor and Sister Rosemary is, he calls her one of the only people who, in his words, "scares the shit" out of him.[1]

You, Smooth and Tough

As a leader, you need to be a persuasive communicator, mixing diplomacy with assertiveness. You've got to get people to do things, without pissing them off in the process.

In other words, you've got to be a Velvet Hammer: smooth enough not to cause resentments, yet forceful enough to inspire action. Good communication requires that *what* you say is balanced against *how* you say it. Again, humility and confidence are at work. Diplomacy involves being thoughtful and respectful in your word choices. It helps to have humility. Assertiveness involves being forthright and direct, which takes confidence. If you're all diplomacy, your message may get watered down and you may come off as a Weakling. If you're overly assertive, you'll be seen as a Pighead and you'll leave people with hurt feelings and resentments. Being a skilled Velvet Hammer ensures that you are both diplomatic and assertive, which improves your likelihood of influencing people to do things without resistance. Here are a few tips:

> ➤ **Stop the brutality.** Being "brutally honest" shouldn't be a point of pride. Why bring violence to your honesty? Those who brag about being so violently honest are usually arrogant Pigheads who are either oblivious to the hurt they cause people or don't care that they cause it. It only takes a few seconds to be more thoughtful in your word choices, but those few seconds can make a world of difference in lowering the risk that your words will prompt ill will and resentments.

> ➤ **Use receptive leader language.** The words you use will either be met with receptivity or prompt defensiveness. Since effective communication is about getting people to think or do things differently, it's important to use words and phrases that actually get through to people. Here are

some phrases that will add some velvet to your language:

- *How do you view this situation? What are you seeing?*
- *Tell me more about your perspective so I can understand it a little better.*
- *I really want to make sure that we come to the right answer together, so I'd like to hear your insights. What do you think?*
- *I appreciate your perspective. What would be some additional ways to look at this situation?*

➤ **Be precise.** When more hammer than velvet is warranted, be precise with your words. Saying, "It's critical that you and your team deliver this project on time to the client because our contract specifies substantial penalties for late deliveries. For the next two weeks, I need you to call me at 4 p.m. so we can review the daily progress and assess the team's needs," is a ton better than "You need to keep me updated about this project."

➤ **Have a BEER.** Feedback comes in two forms: constructive and destructive. Destructive feedback is drunk with emotion and irrationality. To keep feedback constructive, it helps to follow a framework. Consider the BEER approach, developed by leadership blogger Dan McCarthy:[2]

- **Behavior:** *I notice you've been late delivering your last three reports.*
- **Effect:** *When your reports come in late, it causes a bottleneck for other work that has to be delivered by other people. You're losing credibility with your colleagues.*

- **Expectations:** *For the next six months, I need you to hand-deliver the report to me three days before the previous deadline.*
- **Result:** *Getting the reports consistently delivered on time will help rebuild trust with your colleagues and me.*

The Genuine Faker

Imagine having your team go from five people to eighty in an instant. That's what happened to Mike Calihan, a senior executive with Aldridge Electric Incorporated, a national infrastructure construction company based in Chicago. Mike had been a project manager, managing relatively small electrical projects. He had helped to craft a response to a bid put out by the Illinois Department of Transportation. As he tells it, "It was a long shot, because we hadn't managed a project for this type of work at the scale specified in the bid." Mike had a big-gulp moment when the bid was opened and he saw that Aldridge had won the contract. He was tapped to lead the behemoth project, which meant leading a team that was sixteen times larger than he had ever led before.

As Mike explains it, "At first, I had no idea what the hell I was doing. I was in way over my head, and scared as hell." When asked how he went from being a manager of five people to a leader of eighty, he replied, "Sometimes you have to fake it till you make it. You don't start with the skills; you develop them along the way."

A lot of leadership and organizational development books have started to underscore the importance of authenticity. When you're a leader, the people you're leading want to know that the power that accompanies your leadership hasn't gone to your head. They want to know that you "get" that leadership is a privilege, not an entitlement, and that you still pull up your own britches, just like they do. People want to know that you remember your roots and that you haven't forgotten where you came from. In short, they want to know that you're real.

It's important to remember, though, that leadership is not just a way of being and behaving; it's a *role*. And when you're in the role of leader, you have to *perform* that role. What you display to others sometimes has to be based on what the role calls for and what others need, not what you may actually be feeling. For example, if people are freaking out about a large new acquisition the organization is making, you'll only get them more upset if you freak out too, so concealing your true emotions is important. What you portray and what you're actually feeling may sometimes be at odds. But you don't lead people according to where they are; you lead them according to where they need to go. Often that means that your leadership demeanor needs to counterbalance your followers' demeanor. When people are freaking out, you need to portray confidence and resolve. When people are complacent and apathetic, you need to portray worry and concern. This may not exactly be authentic, but it's what people need and what the role of leader calls for you to portray.

You, Authentically Inauthentic

The trick is not to be so caught up in your leadership role that you look like a Shakespearean thespian. You've still got to be real and unpretentious. When you don't know something, you still have to be honest about it. It's just that you also have to cloak your true feelings every now and then. When you do, you'll often start out with one set of feelings and end with another anyway. At the start of a big hairy project, you may be full of knee-knocking fear— and keeping your anxiety under wraps will serve the project better than if you inject it into everyone else. The more you get into the project, the more the fear will start to lift and confidence will start to grow. Yes, as Mike suggested, after faking it you start to make it.

By the way, feeling like you're faking it will be a predominant feeling throughout your career. It's normal and natural for leaders to have a nagging feeling that *this is the day I'll be found out*. No leader has all the answers to every problem, so it takes a lot of improvisation. You'll be making up a lot of stuff as you go along. As you do, people still need to see you as competent. They don't expect you to have all the answers; they just expect you to not shrink from the questions. You were selected for the role of leader for a reason: to *perform*. That performance goes beyond delivering results. It includes portraying that you know what you're doing, even though you sometimes don't. Here are some tips for being a Genuine Faker:

> ➤ **Let 'em see you.** People need to know that you have a life outside work, just like them. They need to see your nonwork identity. Occasionally share stories from your family life. Let people know what you like to do for fun outside work. Include pictures from your outside-work life in your workspace. Show people who you really are when you step outside the role of leader.

➤ **Plumb your unconfident past.** Think about moments in your career when you felt as if you were in over your head. What was the situation/opportunity, and how did it come about? How did you deal with your lack of confidence? How did your confidence evolve as the situation/opportunity progressed? How transparent was what you were experiencing to others around you? How might you use the lessons from that situation/opportunity as a reference point when you feel over your head in future situations?

➤ **Clarify Point B.** Leadership often involves moving people from Point A to Point B. The behaviors required to be successful at Point B are usually different from those at Point A. As a leader, you have to practice the behaviors that the future requires before others catch on. People take cues from you. Draw a line down a piece of paper and create two headers: Point A and Point B. Differentiate between the behaviors that make a person successful today (Point A) and the behaviors that will make a person successful after they've moved to Point B. Acting as the leader means adopting the Point B behaviors before others do.

*You were selected for the role of leader
for a reason: to perform.*

It takes time and seasoning for a leader to become well versed in the roles of Loyal Rebel, Velvet Hammer, and Genuine Faker. Generally, it takes suffering through a lot of butt kicks for you even to be willing to try on these roles. Thus, while it is true that adopting these roles can prevent butt kicks because they are expressions of genuine confidence and humility at work, adopting them may also be the clearest sign that you've become a leader whose leadership has been tempered, refined, and ultimately strengthened by the butt kicks you received when you were less confident or less humble.

In the book's final section, you'll learn how to kick your own ass so that you stay grounded and humble. You'll learn how the redeeming power of a humbling butt kick can reconnect you to the goodness that has always been inside you. When you focus on being a "good leader"— by leading at the *point of goodness*—your integrity will radiate to others, your leadership impact will grow, and you'll enjoy leading more than you do now.

PART IV

Be Humble, Be Good

Just as you won't stay physically fit without exercising, you won't stay healthy as a leader unless you continually take stock of your leadership impact. The best way to prevent future ass kicks is to keep arrogance and weakness at bay. Doing that means regularly kicking your own ass.

There is a point at which your respect for others and your respect for yourself overlap and strengthen one another; I call this the *point of leadership goodness*. First and foremost, leadership starts with character. You can't be a good leader unless you're a good person, and that means being good to yourself and others.

The final section covers

- ➤ how courage relates to self-awareness and examination,
- ➤ how your growth and development as a leader require you to use purposeful discomfort,
- ➤ why every leader should have at least one chief ego deflator,
- ➤ how to lead from the point of goodness.

The world needs more good leaders. The last section provides tips and approaches to help you be and stay good!

CHAPTER 9

How to Kick Your Own Ass

The first rule of leadership: Everything is your fault.
—Hopper, *A Bug's Life*

W ouldn't it be great if people just agreed with everything you said? Wouldn't life be friction-free if people did exactly what you wanted? Wouldn't things go swimmingly if the world revolved around you? Wouldn't it be great if, instead of kicking your butt, people tended to your rosy rump by carrying you around on large cushiony pillows? Ah, the life you could lead if people would just cater to your every demand, agree with all of your opinions, and continually give your ego all the applause that it deserves.

A world devoid of ass kicks, unfortunately, exists only in your sweet dreams. Your concerns mean little to a world that is so worried about itself.

The first law of leadership is this: it's not about you. Leadership is about the people and the organization you're leading. The more you focus on others, the better you'll do. The value of a good psychological butt kicking is that it humbles you into getting over yourself. It deflates your ego so you can more earnestly focus on others instead of yourself. Butt kicks are important ego-reducing events. They are so important that, if your ego hasn't been adjusted in a while, you should put on your boots and kick your own ass.

Need additional reasons? How about because soberly evaluating and challenging your own leadership effectiveness is a great way to prevent the embarrassment of having others kick your leadership butt? Or because the people who report to you deserve for you to be striving to do a better job of leading them? Or because self-awareness is the starting point of healthy leadership change? Besides, while it may be impossible to, say, lick your own elbow, you don't have to be a contortionist to kick your own backside. Below are some suggestions on how to do it.

The first law of leadership is this: It's not about you.

Start with Courage

Aristotle called courage the "first virtue"—because it makes all the other virtues possible. The great writer and theologian C. S. Lewis said courage isn't just one of the virtues, it's all of the virtues taken to the testing point. The Catholic Church deems courage one of the four "cardinal virtues" (joining prudence, temperance, and justice). Courage has always been one of the most important of all life's virtues. It is an essential organizational virtue, too. Courage is just as important inside work as outside it. More importantly, courage is the first virtue of leadership, for it is courage that gives leadership its backbone, resiliency, and resolve.

Jim Kouzes and Barry Posner, authors of many leadership books, including *The Leadership Challenge*, said plainly, "Leadership doesn't happen without courage."[3] They're right. Think of all the ways that courage connects to leading others. Leaders have to render decisions that some people will resist, which takes courage. Leaders have to nudge people outside their comfort zones so they continue to grow, which takes courage (for those being nudged and the leader who is doing the nudging). Leaders have to apply their courage in other ways too, like incessantly challenging the status quo, elevating standards, marshaling resources, balancing competing needs and agendas, developing successors, creating opportunities, and getting results. While they're doing all these things, leaders also have to embody and uphold principles, values, and ideals. They have to be role models of courageous behaviors for others.

It helps to be deeply committed to leading with courage before you can kick your own ass. Here are some questions that leaders answer in my company's Courageous Leadership workshops:

➤ In what ways are you playing it too safe? Why? How might that safety be holding back your career or leadership influence? What courageous actions can you take to counteract the impact of playing it too safe too often?

➤ Courage for the sake of what? How would acting with courage strengthen your leadership and/or enhance your life?

➤ What was the last best mistake you made? What was the last best mistake you rewarded someone else for making?

➤ When was the last time you did something for the first time? How long has it been since you learned something new? What is something new you could try this week?

Employ Purposeful Discomfort

A leader's primary job is to make people uncomfortable. That's because people and organizations don't grow in a zone of comfort. They grow, progress, and evolve in a zone of discomfort. By nudging people into discomfort, leaders prevent apathy and complacency from setting in, while ensuring the growth and development of new skills and abilities. Also, change, by its nature, is an uncomfortable thing, and leaders are charged with bringing about change. When a leader attends to this essential job of making people uncomfortable, in a way that doesn't stoke fear or anxiety, people will eventually learn to become comfortable with discomfort. But this responsibility extends beyond the people the leader is leading. The first person whom the leader needs to make uncomfortable is him- or herself.

Virginia "Ginni" Rometty, the CEO of IBM, said, "Growth and comfort don't coexist." If you want to have a vibrant career, you have to swim out where your toes no longer touch the sand. Rometty herself, before becoming CEO, had a history of purposely taking on new roles that eclipsed her current skills, thus ensuring that she'd grow and develop while learning many aspects of the business. Eventually, given her well roundedness and penchant for figuring out how to be successful while uncomfortable, she became the logical choice to succeed her predecessor, Sam Palmisano.[4]

A leader's primary job is to make people uncomfortable. People and organizations don't grow in a zone of comfort. They grow, progress, and evolve in a zone of discomfort.

As a leader, one good way to ensure your own relevancy is to occasionally shake up your own career. By "shaking up" I don't mean incrementally adding on responsibilities or taking on a few more direct reports. Every three or four years more courageous action is needed to reinvigorate your spirit and keep your leadership talents fresh. Such things as volunteering to chair your organization's community service event, seeking a position in another division, joining a nonprofit board, or moving to another region all qualify. More rarely, leaving an organization you've outgrown is the shake-up that's needed. The point is to purposefully get uncomfortable so that you keep growing and evolving as a leader.

At any moment, most leaders are either contemplating a bold work move or actually in the midst of one. How about you? What bold move are you considering or actually taking? More importantly, will the bold move cause you to be uncomfortable enough to grow? Use the continuum here to gauge how uncomfortable the bold move makes you feel. Only you can decide how much discomfort you're willing to absorb. But if your bold move doesn't make you all that uncomfortable, it's probably not really a bold move. You might need to shake things up by doing something even bolder!

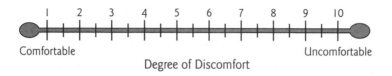

Degree of Discomfort

Appoint a Chief Ego Deflator

When you're in a leadership role, people tend to coddle you too much. It's important for every leader to have kinship with a few key people who won't pamper you. Here's a story from my own life to illustrate the point: One day I bounded upstairs from my office and gleefully showed my wife a picture of me in *TD Magazine*, the industry trade publication of the Association for Talent Development (TD .org). I was being featured as a keynote speaker at one of its conferences. Then I flipped past another couple of pages and showed her another picture of me! It turned out that I was speaking at *two* different conferences. As I looked at her with my "I have arrived" face, she slowly started to grimace, and then, in that disgusted way that seems so universally spousal, she said, "Go clip your nose hairs!" All the hot air that had filled my head quickly dissipated.

Everybody needs somebody who will keep his or her ego in check. You need that special someone who can hold up the mirror so you can catch yourself being yourself. You need at least one person who can call bullshit on your trickery and self-deception. Love that person. Cherish that person. Give that person latitude to kick your fanny freely. That person can keep your ego from raging and your

KICKASS COMEBACKS:
Fire-and-Brimstone Edition

Few churches are as reviled in the United States as the Westboro Baptist Church. Congregants aren't just apocalypse-expecting traditionalists; they're hatred-spewing ideologues who are infamous for picketing the funerals of returning soldiers while carrying signs with homophobic messages such as "God hates fags." The fringe church is not officially affiliated with any religious institution, but considers itself "primitive Baptist" and is anti-Jew, anti-Catholic, anti-Muslim, anti–American soldier, and most especially anti-LGBTQ.

Westboro was founded by Fred Phelps, who, before starting the church, had been a Democrat and a civil rights lawyer. But one day, his two grandsons, both under ten years old, were allegedly propositioned by some allegedly homosexual men at a local park in Topeka, Kansas, where the church is based. Phelps appealed to the city council to do something. Dissatisfied with the inaction, he started picketing, and enlisted his family to do the same. Before long, his protests grew more bigoted and vitriolic. It was under these circumstances that Libby Phelps-Alvare, Fred Phelps's granddaughter, grew up as a committed member of the church. During one protest, at a soldier's funeral, she held a sign that read, "Thank God for dead soldiers."

Libby lived a cloistered existence as a Westboro member, but slowly she was getting glimpses of the outside world and the sanity it offered. She entered a PhD program at the University of Kansas Medical Center, studying physical therapy. She started developing friendships, even with one person whom she suspected was gay. He didn't seem evil.

After returning from a protest trip to Puerto Rico, thirty church members conducted an intervention, severely chastising Libby for wearing a bikini at the beach. She had better change her evil ways, they said, or, like the gays, she would go to hell! For the first time, Libby was on the receiving end of the church's deranged righteousness.

Libby grew intolerant of intolerance. Two days after the intervention, she snuck out of her house and left the church for good. She knew in her heart that you can't really call yourself a Christian if you're praying for people to die, which Westboro members often did.

Libby completely denounced the church and its profane beliefs, but for a while, she felt that God hated her. Slowly, though, that feeling lifted, and as it did, she started to feel less threatened by the world—and more open to it. A Holy Shift was taking place. One way to define leadership is as using one's influence for the good of others. Today, Libby is an advocate for the LGBTQ community, and is now affiliated with Planting Peace, a nonprofit organization that built a rainbow-colored house directly across the street from the Westboro church. She says, "I still believe in God. I just think he's more forgiving."

Sources: Libby Phelps-Alvare, "I Left Westboro—and Now I'm Fighting for Gay Equality," *New York Post*, April 16, 2013, http://nypost.com/2013/04/16/i-left-westboro-and-now-im-fighting-for-gay-equality/; Curtis Wong, "Westboro Baptist Church Founder's Granddaughter Libby Phelps Poses for NOH8 Campaign," *Huffington Post*, June 6, 2014, http://www.huffingtonpost.com/2014/06/12/libby-phelps-noh8-campaign-_n_5488923.html.

humility from falling asleep. We all need someone who can let us know when our nose hairs are getting too long.

Keeping Your Bum Sore

Leaders like the bottom line, so here it is: the more you kick your own ass, the less others will have to. Use the tips in this chapter as a sort of ongoing regimen to ensure that you stay self-aware and grounded in humility. The end result is that you'll become more focused on doing more good for the people you're charged with leading. Here are a few other ways to deliberately put your boot to your bum:

> ➤ **Hire a leadership coach.** Great musicians and athletes have coaches, so why shouldn't you? A coach can help you close the gap between the leader you are and the leader you aim to be.
> ➤ **Seek sobering feedback.** Going through a 360-degree leadership feedback survey process can be a great way to stay self-aware. As long as you don't cherry-pick the people who rate you, you'll draw value from the experience. It helps to have a qualified coach review the results with you because the feedback often stings.
> ➤ **Use a mantra.** Your self-talk as a leader should be geared toward keeping your ego in check. Throughout the day, it's good to remind yourself that your focus as a leader should be on those whom you're leading. Mentally say to yourself, "It's not about me!" or "Get over yourself!"
> ➤ **Go where the leaders are.** How can you be a good leader if you don't get educated about leadership? A simple Google search will help you find many great leadership gatherings and conferences where you can learn more about leadership while interacting with other leaders. One of my favorites is the *Fortune Magazine* Leadership Summit.
> ➤ **Follow more.** Every leader should have at least one community where they can blend in without

fanfare. Even if you're a strong "director" type, having a place where you can step down from the leadership podium is important. Serve in ways that you don't have to stand out. Be the basket passer at church, or the pancake flipper at the charity breakfast, or the weed picker at the garden club. Being a good follower will help you be a more grounded leader.

CHAPTER 10

Leading at the Point of Goodness

If you could kick the person in the pants responsible for most of your trouble, you wouldn't sit for a month.

—Theodore Roosevelt

Where Good Leadership Starts

Leadership, as a topic, can be perplexing. As a leader, you are expected to be bold *and* calculated, passionate *and* reasonable, rational *and* emotional, driven *and* patient, principled *and* flexible, competitive *and* cooperative, strategic *and* tactical, and yes, confident *and* humble. Faced with all of these often conflicting factors, it's enough to make you scratch your head and wonder, *Where on earth do I start?*

In my work with emerging leaders, I hear the question a lot. New leaders, especially, are flummoxed by all the divergent advice they get about what they should focus on to be a good leader. My advice to new leaders is simple: good leadership starts by being good. When it comes to the two words "good leader," the first word brings about the second. You want to be a good leader? First concentrate on being a good person.

Be Good, for Goodness' Sake

Leadership is an inside job. Before you can lead people outwardly, you have to lead yourself inwardly. Leadership starts with internal goodness, in other words, integrity. Goodness is not some pie-in-the-sky philosophical concept. It's not some prudish, goody-two-shoes standard of stilted perfection. Goodness is *practical*. When you're good, people trust you. They know you won't cheat them, or violate their confidences, or mistreat them. They know you'll consider their interests, listen deeply and share generously, and be respectful. Your goodness is the single most important determinant of whether followers will trust your leadership, and trust is crucial to good leadership. When people trust you, they'll work harder on your behalf, they'll have a higher tolerance for your idiosyncrasies, they'll be loyal to you, and, most importantly, they'll act with integrity too. Trust begets trust, and when you act with goodness it becomes an invitation for others to act with theirs, mutually strengthening the trust between you.

You want to be a good leader? First concentrate on being a good person.

Most of us think we're good people, but we also tend to be more forgiving of ourselves when our goodness is compromised. How would you stack up, for example, against the concept of cash register honesty? Imagine driving to work tomorrow morning and stopping to get some coffee on the way. If, after driving a mile down the road, you realize that the cashier inadvertently gave you ten dollars too much in change, would you turn around and drive back? What if turning around meant that you'd be a little late for a meeting? What if the meeting was with your boss? What if the cashier had been a little snotty to you?

Valuing Goodness

It's hard to be good if you haven't defined the values that make up your goodness. Being good means living congruently with your values, and doing that requires actually knowing what your values are. Thus, it's a good idea for all leaders, new and seasoned, to take stock of what they stand for and against:

➤ Which values do you hold most dear?

➤ Which values are nonnegotiable and define a boundary that you will always uphold?

➤ Which values do you think you most embody?

➤ Which values do you lack or most need to develop?

➤ Are you living and working in alignment with your values? How do you know?

When you live in congruence with a clear set of values, your motives, words, and actions come to embody your personal *integrity*. We know a good leader when we see one. There's a certain consistency, fairness, and reasonability in her behavior. We have her full presence when we engage with her. She treats us as a fellow human being, even when she is rungs above us on the organizational ladder. We never feel small around her. We aren't afraid to approach her or ask her a question. We know she respects us and herself. When we move into a leadership role, we refer back to the model she set—how she carried herself, how she weighed and made decisions, and how she treated us and others. We hope to be as good as her someday.

Likewise, we know a not-so-good leader when we see one. It shows up when she inconsistently applies company rules, favors one employee over another, or refuses to concede a lost point. We hear it in her snide, curt, or abrasive comments. We feel it in her transmission of stress and anxiety, causing us to tiptoe around her for fear of setting her off. Sure, we hear her recite a set of values, but she mostly acts outside them. We've experienced a less-than-good leader when, after spending time with her, we feel smaller, less capable, and less sure of our place in the organization. She makes us feel more afraid and less confident. We do, of course, learn a very important lesson from a leader like this: how not to lead.

It Ain't Easy Being Good

Leaders confront situations that tempt them to compromise goodness all the time. Taking the high road may be the right thing, but the uphill gradient also makes it the hard road. When you're faced with a never-seems-to-deliver employee, or a throw-you-under-the-bus peer, or a make-you-kick-your-dog boss, the low road looks mighty attractive. Faced with such all-too-common stressors, the path of least resistance is to yield to the temptation, making compromises that erode your leadership goodness and move you into your all-too-human selfishness. *They aren't being good, so why should I be?* you start to reason. At this point all of those things that make up good leadership—embodying values, emotional maturity, being a role model, inspiring others—start to become conditional: *I'll work on becoming a better leader just as soon as all of these frustrations go away!*

That's not to say that if your leadership has strayed from goodness you can't reclaim it. You can. Often the path a leader follows goes from good to bad and back to good. Provided, of course, something intervenes that causes you to take stock of the leader you really are, not the leader you may be trying to portray to others. An ass kick can become the pivot point at which you get back on the path to goodness because it spurs your awareness that your leadership isn't as good as you thought. Often the most authentic and influential leaders are those whose butt kicks caused them to reclaim their leadership goodness after having gotten diverted into bad.

For example, I once attended the funeral of a former senior vice president (SVP) of HR whose excessive drinking had contributed to his divorce and severely undercut his career. After observing the SVP embarrass himself at a number of company outings, including one incident where he passed out in the driver's seat of his car, the SVP's boss confronted him, telling him that unless he agreed to enter a treatment center, which the company would pay for, he would lose his job. It was just the kick in the pants that the SVP needed to turn his life and career around. He entered rehab, exited a month later, and started earnestly working a twelve-step program. Not only was he able to keep his job, but he ended up having a wonderful leadership career: inside and outside the company. By the time he died, some twenty years later, he was sponsoring forty men in AA who were on their own road to recovery. At his funeral, the church was overflowing with people who had been touched by his reclaimed goodness.

Unfortunately, there are no recovery programs for mediocre, compromised, or bad leaders. There are no fancy treatment centers for Pigheads and Weaklings either. Left unaddressed, the leader who is intimidating, or manipulative, or controlling, or wishy-washy, or ethically fickle will only become more so. A leadership kick in the ass can instigate true leadership transformation, giving you the opportunity to reclaim your goodness, gain humility, and become active in helping others succeed. After all the leadership lessons from a humiliating kick take hold, your fidelity to being a good leader becomes unconditional. You realize that stressors, frustrations, and temptations come with the leadership territory, and don't provide justification to compromise your values and ideals. You learn that you need to be good not in spite of vexing challenges, but to be strong enough to meet them. The redeeming power of a humbling butt kick is that it reconnects you to the goodness that has always existed at your core. You *are* a good person, and that means you *can be* a good leader. Thank God for butt kicks!

> *Left unaddressed, the leader who is intimidating,*
> *or manipulative, or controlling, or wishy-washy,*
> *or ethically fickle will only become more so.*

Aretha Is Right

So much about goodness comes down to how well you treat yourself and others. Goodness is a function of both, but it starts with how you treat yourself. Do you do self-respectful things like stay fit, eat right, set aside "me time," and invest in your own development? Or, conversely, do you smoke, replace working out with excuses, eat fast crap, never make time for yourself, and neglect your own development? Who would you rather work for, a leader who respects him- or herself or one who doesn't value him- or herself enough to practice self-care?

If you treat yourself respectfully, it will be easier to be respectful of others. Respecting others, when you're in a leadership role, is more than just the right thing to do; it's the practical thing to do. When you treat the people you're leading respectfully, they'll be more committed to you and the work that they're tasked with doing. What does treating people with respect involve? Soliciting, valuing, and following their input. Dedicating one-on-one time with them so you are aware of their concerns, struggles, and career aspirations. Being loyal to them, especially when others are blaming or scapegoating them. It also involves being crystal clear about your expectations, leveling with people, and providing frequent feedback about their performance. Treating people with respect also means believing in them and letting them know you do. Who would you rather work for, a leader who treats you this way or one who doesn't? More importantly, how would the people who work for you say you treat them?

Leadership blooms and flourishes when you treat yourself and others really well. I call this the point of leadership goodness. It's the point at which confidence and humility merge; you believe in yourself, you believe in others, and you believe that everyone matters. When you lead from this place, you're leading with character, decency, fairness, and emotional health. Everyone deserves to be led from this place. Aretha Franklin was right: we all appreciate a little R-E-S-P-E-C-T.

The Integration

The biggest lesson that this book has to offer may be this: you get your ass kicked, mostly, when you deserve to. Bad leadership results in butt kicks. What makes a leader good comes down to how well he integrates the lessons from the times when he behaved badly. Though the kick came from another person or event, you might as well have kicked yourself. Arrogance, conceit, and heavy-handedness are repulsive in a leader, but oh so common. So too are timidity, hesitancy, and weakness. Because those bad leadership attributes are common, butt kicks are common too. But if you integrate the lessons by carrying them forward in your future behavior, the result is good leadership.

The beauty of a butt kick, after you integrate the lessons, is that it gives your leadership richness, dimensionality, and perspective. Now your leadership will be free of

KICKASS COMEBACKS: Presidential Edition

Perhaps no man was ever less qualified to become vice president of the United States than Chester A. Arthur. He had never been elected to public office, and he was widely viewed as a political hack. He had even gotten fired from his job as the collector of customs of the Port of New York as the result of a corruption investigation. At the time it was the highest-paying job in the entire government of the United States.

What Arthur did have was a powerful friend: Senator Roscoe Conkling, the ruthless boss of the New York Republican Party. It was Conkling who had placed Arthur in the lucrative customs house job. With a presidential election right around the corner, Conkling now needed to put a check on reform-minded Republican candidate James Garfield. He would make a deal with Garfield: accept Arthur as your running mate, and I'll ensure that you get all of New York's electoral votes. Arthur was a member of the Stalwarts, the antireform faction of the Republican Party, and with Arthur on the ticket, Garfield got the Republican nomination and went on to win the presidency. With Arthur as VP, Conkling had his antireform lackey in place to protect his interests. Arthur would actually live in Conkling's home until inauguration day.

Then something terrible happened: Garfield was shot by a lunatic who exclaimed, "I am a Stalwart of the Stalwarts. . . . Arthur is president now!" For a time, as Garfield lingered on his deathbed (he lingered on for three months), both Conkling and Arthur were suspects. Newspaper headlines also harped on how ill prepared Arthur was to lead, and how he was sure to carry out Conkling's bidding by blocking any government reforms.

Then something wonderful happened: Arthur got reconnected to his goodness. He received a letter from Julia Sand, a bedridden, nearly deaf invalid who, unbeknownst to Arthur, had followed the arc of his career. In her first letter, she described herself as "a poor little woman" who would have no comfort in life unless she could "scold some very big man." Sand would become Arthur's truth teller, redirector, and conscience. Her letters were like much-needed kicks to Arthur's sizable presidential behind. "The people are bowed in grief," she said, "not so much because he is dying, but because you are his successor."

As tough as Sand's letters often were, they appealed to Arthur's better self. She *believed* in Arthur's goodness when nearly everyone else in the country didn't. "Great emergencies," she wrote, "awaken generous traits which have lain dormant half a life. If there is a spark of true nobility in you, now is the occasion to let it shine." She continued, "Do what is more difficult and brave. Reform!"

Arthur's father was a Baptist minister and outspoken abolitionist. Arthur had gone on to become a lawyer, carrying his father's abolitionist values forward. One of his clients was Elizabeth Jennings Graham, an African American civil rights pioneer who had been denied a seat on a streetcar because she was black. The case, which Arthur won, led to the desegregation of the entire New York City transit system.

The twenty-three letters that Sand wrote Arthur during his presidency served to reconnect him to the goodness he had inside him, prodding him to lead from his more noble self. To the frustration of Conkling and the party establishment, Arthur would go on to vigorously fight the corrupt practices and patronage system that had elevated him to power. As president, unlike when he was the collector of customs, Arthur would never use his leadership power to enrich himself. Instead, he instituted dramatic civil service reforms, vetoed pork barrel projects, and outlawed the till-then-common practice of extracting campaign contributions from government workers in order for them to keep their jobs.

Historians now believe that Sand's letters proved pivotal in Arthur's transformation from a political sycophant to a capable chief executive. The letters were so important to him that he kept them in a special file that wasn't discovered until 1958.

It's really a remarkable kickass leadership comeback. A small disabled woman who was not legally allowed to vote reconnected the president of the United States to his inner goodness and, in the process, transformed his presidency and the nature of government employment. What qualified her to advise a president? Citizenship, love of country, common sense, and personal integrity. Simply put: leadership.

Sources: Lillian Cunningham, "The Redemption of President Chester A. Arthur," podcast, *Washington Post*, May 29, 2016, https://www.washingtonpost.com /news/on-leadership/wp/2016/05/29/the-redemption-of-president-chester-a -arthur/; James Marshall, "Ethics Tales: How Julia Sand Saved a President and Changed a Nation," *Ethics Alarms*, March 6, 2015, https://ethicsalarms.com/2015 /03/06/ethics-tales-how-julia-sand-saved-a-president-and-changed-the-nation/.

the encumbrances of self-doubt or self-absorption. You'll be better able to relate to the idiosyncrasies and imperfections of others because you know they reflect your own. You'll make decisions based on principles, not on expediency or convenience. You'll pay close attention to the needs and aspirations of others, listening as an ally who genuinely cares about their interests. You'll have more empathy, tolerance, and humility. All of which, surprisingly, strengthen your leadership impact. The more impact your leadership has, the more genuine confidence you'll gain. You'll become a good leader by drawing on the lessons you integrated from any bad you once did.

Getting Good

The world needs more good leaders. That means the world needs you to be a good leader too. Most especially, *you* need you to be a good leader. Leading with goodness is a healthy way to lead. The more centered on being a good leader you are, the less likely you are to get your butt kicked. Enhancing your goodness is a function of acting with integrity, gratitude, and selflessness. It involves being attuned to how people and situations affect your emotions, and not letting them drive your responses. It means being able to feel your feelings without acting while you're inebriated by them.

In the end, leadership is about what works. And what works for today's leaders are the same things that worked for the good leaders of yesterday. Passion, vision, respect, character, backbone, humility, and hard work are blessedly old and wonderfully contemporary leadership concepts. If you center your leadership on those things, your leadership will do a lot of good.

If you're not up for getting good as a leader, it's best that you step aside. Too much bad has already been done to the world by disrespectful leaders; there's no need to add to the damage. My bet, though, is that you are committed to doing whatever you can to be a really good leader; otherwise, you wouldn't have read the book all the way through. What follows are ten final tips for keeping your words honest, your motives pure, and your leadership good. Use them to prevent future butt kicks or to treat the butt kicks you may have recently endured. But use them. They'll help you be the good leader your people want and the world needs.

➤ **Start from bad.** Getting good starts by exploring your bad. Review your career regrets. Think of situations or interactions for which you wish you had a do-over. Why do you regret how you behaved? What does how you behaved say about you and your humanness? What about you would you like to change? How would making those changes benefit your leadership impact?

➤ **Conduct a kick review.** List all the butt kicks you've gotten over your career. What was the situation? Who kicked you? How did you contribute to the kick? What themes emerge from all the kicks you've gotten? What lessons did you draw from the kicks, and how have they impacted your leadership?

➤ **Invite feedback.** The best way to prevent obliviousness is to get feedback. Think of it as initiating your own butt kicking. If your organization has a 360-degree feedback process, ask to go through it. If not, send a simple e-mail to people whose input you would trust. Don't cherry-pick. Pick people who are truthful with you. Ask/say the following:
  ◆ What do you see as my leadership strengths?
  ◆ Share an example of when you think I did a good job of leading.
  ◆ Share an example of when I missed the opportunity to lead in the way that I could have.
  ◆ What suggestions can you offer for helping me improve my leadership?

➤ **Hang out with good people.** Spend more time with good leaders you admire. Notice how they process decisions, handle stress, and treat people. What about their goodness is worth mimicking? Ask them to share their leadership stories with you. What hardships did they endure? What obstacles did they overcome? What butt kicks did they get and what did they learn from them? How did they get to be the leaders they are today? What advice do they have for you to be a good leader?

➤ **Bring good to bad.** When facing crappy situations or people who are behaving badly, show up with your own goodness. Not by being self-righteous or holier-than-thou, but by being authentic. Disarm people by acknowledging your imperfections or sharing a story about a time when you got it wildly wrong. Listen a lot. Then let them know that you'd like to help make the situation better. By acting like an adult, you just might call forth the adult in them.

➤ **Fess up.** When you're wrong, promptly admit it. Genuine contrition disarms people fast. Plus, when you're honest about your mistakes, people learn that they can trust you. Provided, of course, that you don't keep making the same mistake.

➤ **Develop a leadership point of view (POV).** Think for yourself. At least once a week, disconnect from all of your electronic tethers. Pick a hot topic of conversation or major decision that's currently being evaluated in your organization. What is *your* point of view? How is your POV similar to or different from others'? How could you share your POV with others, confidently and humbly?

➤ **Lead from a high road.** Lead respectfully. Treat people with decency, courtesy, and diplomacy.

Power does not entitle one to be unkind. When faced with unyielding pressure, or high stress, or obnoxious people, stooping lower won't make you more effective—but it will make you regretful. When the going gets tough, seek higher ground.

➤ **Be good to others.** Leadership is not about the leader; it's about those being led. Your job as a leader is to leave the organization better off than you found it, and the people better off than you found them. You get the former by doing the latter. Get focused on improving the conditions of those you're leading. Constantly strive to create opportunities for them to grow, develop, and excel. Ask yourself, *What are their needs and how can I fulfill them? What are their points of pain and how can I help alleviate them? What kind of leadership do they need from me?*

➤ **Be good to yourself.** If you want to be a good leader, be good to yourself. Remember these two words: *personal fidelity*. Be faithful to taking care of yourself. Make time for fun, play, and just *being*. Get coaching if you need to lose weight, stop smoking, or get in shape. Treating yourself well is the first sign of self-respect. And, hey, if you don't respect yourself, why should you expect others to respect you?

The world needs more good leaders. That means the world needs you to be a good leader too. Most especially, you need you to be a good leader. Leading with goodness is a healthy way to lead.

Finally, it helps to remember that you are the only person with whom you will spend your entire life. From your first inhale to your last exhale, you are the soul you will always be with. Being someone worth spending time with is supremely important. Being comfortable in your own skin is a function of always trying to do the next right thing, especially when it's hard. It's okay to mess up, be imperfect, and backslide. It's normal to occasionally get angry, be irritable, or be irrational. All of those things make you human. But what also makes you human is the ability to notice when you're off-center, or recommit to a higher standard after you've taken a low road, or apologize when you've harmed or hurt someone.

Becoming a better you will help you better serve others. It will also help you live in your own skin with confidence, contentment, and gratitude. It is the constant striving to be better, then, that defines your humanity, your goodness, and your leadership. In the end, your integrity is ultimately what will bring confidence and humility to your leadership. It is in everyone's best interest that you be a good leader. So be good. And lead.

Notes

1. Joel Reece, "Chicagoans of the Year 2014: Sister Rosemary Connelly," *Chicago Magazine*, November 17, 2014, http://www.chicagomag.com/Chicago-Magazine/December-2014/Chicagoans-of-the-Year-2014-Rosemary-Connelly/.

2. Dan McCarthy, "Tough Feedback Tips," *Great Leadership*, February 16, 2008, http://www.greatleadershipbydan.com/2008/02/tough-feedback-tips.html.

3. James M. Kouzes and Barry Z. Posner, *Finding the Courage to Lead* (Hoboken, NJ: Wiley, August 2013), 63.

4. Jena McGregor, "IBM Sets an Example with Ginni Rometty—and Not Just by Selecting Her as Its First Female CEO," *Washington Post*, October 26, 2011, https://www.washingtonpost.com/blogs/post-leadership/post/ibm-sets-an-example-with-ginni-rometty--and-not-just-by-selecting-her-as-its-first-female-ceo/2011/04/01/gIQArCqwIM_blog.html.

Acknowledgments

This book is only possible because of some pretty amazing clients. Over the course of twenty-five years, I have been lucky to have been brought into some unique client situations, most of which required strong leadership to resolve. I love my clients. They have enriched my life and provided me with a fulfilling career. Without them, I wouldn't know jack about leadership. A few clients have been particularly stellar, including Ken Aldridge, board chair of Aldridge Electric Incorporated; Dan and Matt Walsh, co-CEOs of Walsh Construction; and Dan Plote, CEO of Plote Construction. I'm also thankful for having worked with, and learned from, many leaders and managers at all three companies.

While I appreciate clients who have taken a risk on me by bringing me in to work with their leaders, I especially appreciate clients who take risks *with* me. Clients who are willing to experiment and cocreate are my favorite kind. Steve Rivi, the CEO of Aldridge Electric Incorporated, to whom this book is dedicated, is at the top of the list. We've developed some great leadership programs together. Other folks who have taken many giant leaps with me include Mike Calihan, Chris Kennebeck, Stacy McNeil, Jerry Reece, Krista Roberts, and Renea Scoble. Finally, over the last decade, I've spent the most time thinking about leadership with Craig Atkinson, VP of Communication and

Strategic Services at Walsh Construction. The leadership workshops and keynotes that we've delivered have been especially gratifying. Thanks for being a great friend and colleague.

Giant Leap Consulting is a courage-building company, and I draw courage from the good people who work with the company, including Justine Foo, Sara Gee, Becky Jarrell, Charles Lang, Ahli Moore, Matt Watson, and a host of other independent trainers and consultants.

In 2003, back before I had gray hair, Steve Piersanti, president of Berrett-Koehler Publishers, took a shot on me and published my first book, *Right Risk*. Anyone who has had the good fortune of working with Steve knows what an impressive and courageous guy he is. He epitomizes the "good leader" I described in the last chapter of this book. I am thankful for our friendship, and for the other good people who have been drawn into my universe because of him. Neal Maillet, editorial director, instigated and developed this book. He's not only a sharp thinker, he's a fast processor. Our conversations are always amped up with positive electricity. Jeevan Sivasubramaniam, editorial managing director and resident curmudgeon, always brings a fresh perspective and great ideas. I like to think that the iconoclastic nature of this book drew an extra dose of his love, humor, and book-enhancing skepticism. Thank you, Neal and Jeevan, along with the rest of the Berrett-Koehler staff, for being great professionals and good peeps. My thanks extend to the four people whom Berrett-Koehler enlisted as part of the book's review process: Nic Albert, Britt Bravo, Andrea Chilcote, and Chris Morris. Thanks for kicking my ass . . . in a good way.

Nancy Breuer and I worked together on my previous book, *Leaders Open Doors*. She's the founder of Clear Magic, and I wouldn't think of writing another book without her excellent editing and coaching skills. Thanks, Nancy!

For a number of years, the social media publicity team at Weaving Influence has been helping me spread the good word on courage building and leadership. Special thanks to Becky Robinson and Christy Kirk for your leadership.

People who know me from my keynotes and workshops only get to see my pulsing extroversion. The writer side of me is very different. I am a cloisterer. I can't write a single word if there's a lot of commotion around me. So while I am writing, I close my office door, turn off my phone, and shut out the world. That includes shutting out my family for hours on end. Shannon, Alex, Bina, and Ian, in case it sometimes doesn't look that way, I hope you all know that there are no people in this universe with whom I'd rather be traveling through time than all of you. I love you all. A lot, a lot.

My life has been propped up by mentors, role models, and teachers. Their presence in my life has made me a better person and professional. I am eternally grateful to Chip Bell, Elaine Biech, Ken Blanchard, Hines Brannan, Bob Carr, Kevin Eikenberry, B. J. Gallagher, Marshall Goldsmith, Verne Harnish, Sharon Jordan-Evans, Jennifer Kahnweiler, Bev Kaye, Jim Kouzes, Fr. Vince Malatesta, Steve Miller, Conor Neil, Barry Posner, Marcia Reynolds, Pam Schmidt, O. K. Sheffield, Maren Showkeir, Jesse Stoner, Dick Thompson, Michael Wilkinson, and scores of others who have positively impacted my life and career.

Finally, I want to thank all of the people who have read my books or attended my workshops. In your life and work I see and find my own. You inspire me, give me hope for the future, and make me want to be more courageous. Thank you for touching my life with your stories and struggles. I promise to always remember that you are the reason I have a career.

Index

About the Author

Sarah Hooker

Bill Treasurer is the chief encouragement officer of Giant Leap Consulting, a courage-building company that is on a mission to help people and organizations be more courageous so they can drive out fear and produce exceptional results. For over two decades, Bill has worked to help leaders be more courageous, just, and effective.

Bill is the author of *Leaders Open Doors* (ATD Press, 2014), which focuses on the key responsibility leaders have to be opportunity creators. The book became the top-selling leadership training book on Amazon.com in 2014. Notably, Bill donates 100 percent of the royalties from the book to programs that support children with special needs.

Bill is also the author of *Courage Goes to Work* (Berrett-Koehler, 2008), an internationally best-selling book about how to build workplace courage. The book gives practical strategies for inspiring courageous behavior in workplace settings. Bill is also the creator of the world's only do-it-yourself courage-building training program, *Courageous Leadership: Using Courage to Transform the Workplace* (Wiley, 2011). The program promotes leadership courage and has been taught to thousands of executives throughout the world.

Bill's first book, *Right Risk* (Berrett-Koehler, 2003), is about smart risk taking and draws on Bill's experiences as a professional athlete. Bill is a former captain of the U.S. high-diving team and has performed over 1,500 dives from heights over one hundred feet. The book received jacket endorsements from Dr. Stephen R. Covey and Dr. Ken Blanchard, and the front cover features a photo of Bill diving while engulfed in flames!

Bill served as the senior editor of *Positively M.A.D.* (Berrett-Koehler, 2005). Over fifty renowned authors contributed to the book, which encourages readers to put their anger to work by producing good outcomes. Don't be mad, be *positively* mad!

Bill attended West Virginia University on a full athletic scholarship, and received his master's degree from the University of Wisconsin. He served as the board chair of Leadership Asheville, a community-based leadership program run by the University of North Carolina at Asheville.

Bill's most fulfilling role is being Shannon's husband, and the father of Bina, Alex, and Ian, whom he calls his "three heartbeats." After the love of his family, Bill says everything else in his life is just gravy.

About Giant Leap Consulting

Giant Leap Consulting (GLC) is a courage-building company that is on a mission to help people and organizations act with more courage. Since its founding in 2002, GLC has conducted over five hundred client engagements to help individuals and organizations perform at a higher level. Our services include

- ➤ **Courageous future:** Strategic planning to rally the organization around a bold and compelling vision for the future.
- ➤ **Courageous leadership:** Comprehensive leadership development and succession-planning programs for emerging and experienced leaders.
- ➤ **Courageous teaming:** Team-building programs to strengthen and align senior executive teams.
- ➤ **Courageous coaching:** Individual coaching to strengthen the leadership skills of managers and executives.
- ➤ **Courageous development:** Skill-building training workshops for all employees, covering such topics as culture, leading change, professionalism, team leadership, decision making and risk taking, presentation skills, strategic thinking, and many others. We specialize in custom-designed workshops.

Giant Leap is proud of its client list, which includes NASA, Accenture, Lenovo, UBS Bank, Saks Fifth Avenue, CNN, Walsh Construction, Hugo Boss, nCino, Aldridge Electric Incorporated, the Children's Miracle Network, Spanx, Plote Construction, the U.S. Centers for Disease Control and Prevention (CDC), the U.S. Department of Veterans Affairs, and the Pittsburgh Pirates. In addition, through our work with the National Science Foundation, we have facilitated strategic-planning engagements at Harvard University, the Massachusetts Institute of Technology (MIT), the University of California at Berkeley, the University of Southern California, the University of Chicago, Brown University, and many other renowned institutions of higher learning.

To learn more about Bill Treasurer and Giant Leap Consulting, visit our websites: BillTreasurer.com, GiantLeapConsulting.com, CourageBuilding.com, Managerial Courage.com, and LeadersOpenDoors.com. To contact Bill about working with your organization, send an e-mail to info@giantleapconsulting.com or call 800-867-7239. To connect with Bill or Giant Leap through social media, visit Facebook (http://facebook.com/bill.treasurer), Twitter (@btreasurer), and LinkedIn (www.linkedin.com/in/courage).

Berrett–Koehler
Publishers
Connecting people and ideas
to create a world that works for all

Dear Reader,

Thank you for picking up this book and joining our worldwide community of Berrett-Koehler readers. We share ideas that bring positive change into people's lives, organizations, and society.

To welcome you, we'd like to offer you a free e-book. You can pick from among twelve of our bestselling books by entering the promotional code **BKP92E** here: http://www.bkconnection.com/welcome.

When you claim your free e-book, we'll also send you a copy of our e-newsletter, the *BK Communiqué*. Although you're free to unsubscribe, there are many benefits to sticking around. In every issue of our newsletter you'll find

- A free e-book
- Tips from famous authors
- Discounts on spotlight titles
- Hilarious insider publishing news
- A chance to win a prize for answering a riddle

Best of all, our readers tell us, "Your newsletter is the only one I actually read." So claim your gift today, and please stay in touch!

Sincerely,

Charlotte Ashlock
Steward of the BK Website

Questions? Comments? Contact me at bkcommunity@bkpub.com.

MIX
Paper from
responsible sources
FSC® C002589

Certified

Corporation
bcorporation.net